DOUBLE CROSS

DECEPTION
TECHNIQUES
IN WAR

DOUBLE CROSS

Paul B. Janeczko

CANDLEWICK PRESS

First edition 2017

Library of Congress Catalog Card Number pending
ISBN 978-0-7636-6042-0

17 18 19 20 21 22 BVG 10 9 8 7 6 5 4 3 2 1

Printed in Berryville, VA, U.S.A.

This book was typeset in Melior Medium and Stone Sans.

Candlewick Press
99 Dover Street
Somerville, Massachusetts 02144

visit us at www.candlewick.com

For Art Donnelly—
carpenter, painter, handyguy,
sometimes a magician,
and always my brother
from another mother

In memoriam
Louise Hamilton (1953–2016)

CONTENTS

· · · · · · · · · · ·

Deception Basics

Every year as June approaches, news stories commemorate the Allies' 1944 D-day landings in Normandy, France. Some of the stories mention that the landings' success hinged on the intricate and well-executed deception campaign that preceded D-day. That campaign, called Operation BODYGUARD, fooled Hitler into thinking that the invasion would come at Pas-de-Calais, France, about two hundred miles northeast of the real landing site. The deception induced Hitler to shift crucial armor units and a significant number of his troops to Pas-de-Calais. Even after D-day, as Allied forces worked to establish their beachhead in Normandy, Hitler remained so convinced that the *real* invasion was still coming at Pas-de-Calais that he kept his troops there for weeks. Although the war would rage for another year, D-day was a turning point. The days of Hitler and the Third Reich were numbered. And deception had played a key role.

In 1942, the American Joint Chiefs of Staff set up the Joint Security Council to protect the security of information and implement deception operations. The Joint Chiefs of Staff viewed the goals of deception as causing the enemy "to make false estimates and mistakes in his military decisions and consequent actions, thereby contributing to the accomplishments of tasks in our over-all military mission." Deception has, in fact, played a part in every war throughout history. Sometimes its role has been small, but at other times, as in Normandy in 1944, deception has been instrumental in changing the course of a war and, in some cases, changing history.

Many of the principles and techniques of deception in war have remained unchanged throughout history. But as the technologies of war have developed, deception operations have been quick to incorporate the advancements. For example, the development of telegraphy during the American Civil War provided a fast and reliable way to send information. And the fact that intelligence sent over telegraph wires could be intercepted meant that the medium could also be used to send *mis*information. Around the same time, a new mode of travel, the hot-air balloon, began to be adopted for use in reconnaissance, an important component of deception planning. During World War I, the airplane came into its own as an offensive weapon, and it wasn't long before it, too, became a tool of reconnaissance and battlefield damage assessment, both useful in planning deception operations.

The term *deception* actually encompasses two concepts: cover and deception. As defined during World War II by the Joint Security Council, cover activities are "planned measures for disguising or concealing an operation against an objective," whereas deception operations are "planned measures for revealing or conveying to the enemy . . . information . . . regarding our strategic plans, strengths, dispositions, operations for tactics, with the purpose of causing him to reach false estimates and act thereon."

As author Thaddeus Holt has more elegantly put it, "Cover conceals truth; deception conveys falsehood. Cover induces nonaction; deception induces action." Both are geared for a specific result on the part of the adversary. In a World War I example of cover, the Allies camouflaged battlefield observation posts as trees. And Operation BODYGUARD in World War II is a classic example of active deception. Throughout this book, the word *deception* will be used as an umbrella term to refer to both kinds of operations.

Military strategists rely on the following principles when considering their deception tactics:

- **Focus:** While the "customer" of a deception is the intelligence agency to which misleading or false information is directed, its "target" is the enemy commander, because he or she is the one who will make strategic decisions based on the information.
- **Action:** The plan must be designed to make the enemy do something specific that will be of benefit to one's operations.
- **Coordination of Efforts:** Early deceptions were generally initiated by a single person. Roughly at the start of the twentieth century, deception became institutionalized, with more of the work done by

committees and agencies within governments. These groups require coordination to avoid duplication of operations and problems when one agency doesn't know what another is doing.

- **Security:** Deception operations must be kept secret, and they must also ensure the secrecy of the military operations with which they are connected.
- **Credibility:** No matter how good a deception plan is, it will fail if the enemy does not believe that the story it tells is possible. The enemy need not believe that the scenario *will* occur, only that it *could* occur.
- **Adaptability:** The best deceptions are not cookie-cutter operations, in which a tactic that worked in one battle is blindly followed in the next. They are, rather, carefully tailored to the objectives of military forces, the needs of commanders, and the expertise of intelligence agencies.

Deception techniques used by military strategists include:

- **Concealment:** Hiding military assets with available cover, such as trees, bushes, or buildings.
- **Camouflage:** Hiding military assets through artificial means, such as covering an ammunition supply with a net that looks like foliage. In negative (or

passive) camouflage, objects are hidden. In positive (or active) camouflage, dummy military objects are used to mislead the enemy about the strength or placement of assets.

- **Planted False Information:** Feeding false intelligence to the enemy via double agents, news articles, or intentional leaks by diplomats.
- **Demonstration:** Taking actions that indicate preparation for a military action, but without the intent of actually carrying it out.
- **Feint:** A military action designed to draw the enemy out or distract from the main assault. One example is a tactical retreat, carried out in hopes that the enemy will follow and designed to get one's own forces in a better position.
- **Repetitive Process:** A repeated drill or practice maneuver designed to lull the enemy into a false sense of security, making them vulnerable when the drill or practice becomes an actual maneuver.
- **Apparent Bad Luck or Mistake:** Planting false information in such a way that the enemy is fooled into thinking that they have discovered some important intelligence because of an accident or bad luck on the part of the adversary.
- **Substitution:** Replacing something real with something fake or vice versa.

- **The Lure:** Creating a situation the enemy will be drawn into exploiting, only to learn later that it was a trap.
- **The Double Bluff:** One of the riskiest of deceptions, a double bluff allows the enemy to know the truth about an operation in the hope that they will find it "too good to believe" and ignore it.
- **Display:** Making military assets—real, dummy, or a mix of the two—visible to the enemy in order to mislead them about one's strengths, position, or intentions.
- **Ruse:** The wearing of "false colors"—the enemy's uniforms—accompanied by the use of their equipment to makes one's own forces appear to be those of the adversary.

While deception has been practiced in war throughout history, the Allies' deception operations during World War II were remarkable for their breadth, complexity, and overall contribution to the war effort. From code-breaking to a highly successful stable of double agents to Operation BODYGUARD, there is little question that during World War II, the Allies, especially the British, became masters of the game of deception in war.

Since then, deception has played a less central role in conflicts but has still been practiced from time to time. When troops needed relief in the Korean War, both sides covered the change of troops with fake artillery and vehicle noise. And during the Vietnam War, North Vietnamese forces flourished on guerrilla tactics and deception, while the U.S. military viewed battlefield deception as somehow "un-American." But then in the Gulf War of 1991, General Arnold Schwarzkopf used a so-called Hail Mary play to fool the Iraqis into thinking that American troops would be staging a direct attack when, in fact, they planned to attack the Iraqi flanks.

This book will look at some of history's best fake-outs, ploys, lies, and spies, with an eye to the techniques employed and their variations. As you read about these deceptions in times of war, it is important to understand that some of the operations did not always achieve the specific strategic success that the planners had in mind. However, it is equally important to understand that the ops frequently succeeded in planting doubts in the minds of the enemy, doubts that led to hesitation on the battlefield or to a change in plans. You will see that deceptions were often all about showing the enemy what your forces *could* do. After seeing deception in action, you, too, may agree with Sun Tzu, an ancient Chinese general who wrote in *The Art of War* that "All warfare is based on deception."

CHAPTER 1

EARLY DECEPTIONS

One of the earliest stories of deception in battle is the biblical account of Gideon. Gideon's people, the Israelites, had been driven from their land by the Midianites and other eastern tribes and were living in caves in the mountains. Each year, when the Israelites were ready to harvest their grain crop, the Midianites swept through the area, taking what they wanted of the bountiful harvest.

According to the biblical account, Gideon received a message from God, instructing him to gather a force and drive the Midianites out. Daunted but determined, Gideon sent out word that he was looking for warriors. Ten thousand Israelites responded. But, as the story continues, God told Gideon that he had far too many men, so Gideon selected three hundred fighters for the initial assault. He instructed the others to gather to the east and wait.

Gideon leads the Israelites into battle against the Midianites.

Gideon gave each of his three hundred men a lamp, a pitcher, and a trumpet. In the middle of the night, they lit their candles and placed them in the pitchers to hide their light. They then followed Gideon from their hiding place in the mountains and encircled the Midianites' camp. On Gideon's command, the soldiers began to shout, shatter their pitchers, and blow their trumpets. The Midianites, suddenly awakened by the noise, rose in fear and disarray and saw, in the darkness, a circle of lights and swords held high.

In panic, the Midianites fled to the east, toward their homeland. Gideon let them flee, knowing that the remainder of his force was waiting in the valley beyond the camp. The ensuing battle was fierce, but the flustered Midianites, though they far outnumbered the Israelite forces, were no match for Gideon's waiting army. Gideon had used the display technique, making his initial assault force seem much more numerous than it was. He also used the initial assault as a feint, when the main battle was yet to come. Both techniques combined for a successful rout.

Another ancient story of deception is the tale of the Trojan Horse. Although most scholars agree that the story is fictional, it holds a firm place in Latin and Greek mythology. The main ancient source for the story is the *Aeneid,* written by the Roman poet Virgil between 29 and 19 BCE. It's also told in the *Odyssey,* written by the Greek poet Homer about seven hundred years earlier. While the Trojan Horse might be a myth, the Trojan War does have some basis in historical fact and may have been fought between 1200 and 1100 BCE. Embellished or not, the story of the battles between the forces of Greece and Troy makes for great reading. And the tale of the Trojan Horse is another example of deception in war.

The story goes that the Greeks had encircled the walls of Troy and kept the city in a state of siege for some time. The Greek hero Odysseus could see that in order to break the stalemate and defeat the Trojans, the Greek forces needed a way inside the city's formidable walls. Odysseus had an idea. He would build a huge wooden horse. But not just *any* wooden horse. This horse would appear to be a glorious prize of great value, with polished wood and a gilded mane and hooves — a prize the Trojans would surely want to take into their city. And hiding in its belly would be Odysseus and twenty of his most trusted soldiers.

Once the horse had been built, Odysseus and his men climbed inside through a trapdoor. They left their armor behind, for fear that its clanking would give them away. To fulfill their part in Odysseus's plan, the Greek forces burned their camp and set sail, appearing to have given up on the siege. However, they only sailed far enough to hide behind an island in the Aegean Sea, where they could not be seen from the walls of Troy.

The lure worked. When the Trojans saw the Greek fleet in full sail, they emerged from Troy to verify what the lookouts had told them: that the Greeks had given up and sailed for home. Well, not *all* the Greeks had departed. A soldier named Sinon had been left behind with a story to tell the Trojan generals. Appearing angry and fearful, he claimed that Odysseus had decided to offer him as a sacrifice to appease the gods. He said that while his guards slept, he had fled and hidden. He explained that the Greeks had built a great wooden horse as an offering to Athena, the goddess of wisdom and military victory. He added that the Greeks had made it so large — too large to be dragged without great effort within the city's walls — so the Trojans would burn it, thereby bringing the wrath of Athena upon them.

Although the generals listened with interest, Laocoön, a Trojan priest, was not convinced of Sinon's story and uttered an expression that has been used ever since: "Beware of Greeks bearing gifts." The story goes that at the moment he voiced his suspicions, two giant serpents glided toward him and his two children, coiled around them all, and crushed the breath out of them. With no one else voicing any misgivings, the Trojans dragged the gigantic horse through the gates into Troy.

The evening was loud with festivities as the Trojans celebrated the departure of the Greeks. In the meantime, Odysseus and his band of warriors waited in the belly of the horse. Soon, the Trojans fell into deep sleep. Sinon crept from Troy and lit a signal fire atop the tomb of Achilles, calling the Greek fleet to return, which it did, as quietly as the night itself. In

Troy, a rope ladder dropped from the belly of the horse, and Odysseus and his men climbed out. Two of them opened the gates of Troy, and the Greek troops flooded through.

The magnificent Trojan Horse led to the fall of Troy to the Greeks.

The battle was long and fierce, but the element of surprise—a product of the Greeks' deception—had left the Trojans at a disadvantage. For three days, the Greeks plundered the riches of Troy. Some of the Trojans did mount a counterattack, using a deception of their own: putting on the armor of dead Greek soldiers in an attempt to sneak into the enemy's ranks. But this "false colors" strategy proved futile. Troy was lost. The Greeks had deceived the Trojans with two techniques: the camouflage of the Trojan Horse and the planting of false information in the form of Sinon's sob story.

Centuries after the ancient Greeks, a deception technique was one of the decisive factors in the Battle of Hastings, in 1066, a confrontation that changed the history of England. In January of that year, the English king Edward the Confessor died without a clear heir. His brother-in-law, Harold Godwinson, quickly assumed the throne. This move did not sit well with King Harald Hardrada of Norway and Duke William II of Normandy, both of whom laid claim to the English crown. In eleventh-century politics, there was one common way to settle such a dispute: war. The Norwegians invaded England from the north and gained an early victory at Fulford. However, Harold Godwinson's army of paid professional soldiers wielding battle-axes and javelins surprised the Norwegian troops at Stamford Bridge on September 26, 1066, and slaughtered them. The Norwegian king was among the dead.

Two days after Harold Godwinson's triumph, Duke William II of Normandy and his army of five thousand landed on the south coast of England and marched to Hastings, where they made camp. When Harold heard of the invasion, he quickly marched his troops to meet William. Some historians feel that a smarter move for Harold would have been to sit tight in London until he could fully replace the men he had lost at Stamford Bridge. But Harold thought that he could surprise William the way he had surprised King Harald of Norway. William, on the other hand, knew that Harold was "impetuous and bold" and would rush to meet him in battle.

Harold did make a wise strategic move by positioning his troops on high ground, which William could assault only with deadly consequences to his men. Such proved to be the case. Even William's archers were ineffective. Shooting from below, they could not send their arrows with the arching trajectory that was most deadly. Harold's troops, on the other hand, were quite skilled at close-quarters fighting.

The Normans were repulsed in two attempts to dislodge the English troops from their high ground. It was time for William to try a different tactic. He attacked a third time, but then quickly retreated, his troops seemingly in disarray. The English, jubilant at their apparent victory, broke ranks and charged down the hill in pursuit of the Normans. Drawn from their heights, the English had abandoned their strategic advantage. But the Norman retreat was a deception, a feint. Suddenly, the "fleeing" Normans turned and charged the English. Taking full advantage of the now-level battlefield, the Norman archers let fly a deadly storm of arrows. One of them hit Harold in the eye, leaving him mortally wounded.

Seeing their fallen leader, the remaining English troops quickly fled for their lives. The Normans were victorious due to William's feigned retreat. And the world was changed, as England became more connected to western Europe.

English troops are cut down by the archers of Duke William II of Normandy.

But did William really execute a brilliant feigned retreat, or did he just get lucky? Historians are divided on that issue. Some feel that such a "clever stratagem to defeat the English . . . is unlikely." They believe that in the chaos of battle, it would have been difficult to control the troops enough to successfully pull off such a feint. On the other hand, some historians believe that the feigned retreat was a "common tactic in cavalry fighting, but wholly unknown in England." Perhaps what matters most in the consideration of deception in war is the fact that after Hastings, the feigned retreat became a tactic that was used again and again.

Over time, most western European countries engaged in wars with one another, forming assorted alliances, settling old scores, and always looking for ways to gain wealth, power, and land. Fought on North American soil, the French and Indian War (1756–1763) pitted the British against the French and their Native American allies in an extension of hostilities between the two nations that also played out in Europe and on the high seas.

The British wanted to drive the French from North America. After many successes by the French forces in the Ohio Valley and in Canada, the tide of the war changed when William Pitt became England's new secretary of state and adapted English battlefield tactics to fit the New World terrain and environment. In addition, some of the Native American tribes changed sides and fought with the British. The French found themselves with two outposts: Fort Carillon (later called Ticonderoga), in upstate New York, and the city fortress of Québec. When Carillon fell to British forces, Pitt's men turned their attention to Québec, an "almost impregnable fortress" on the cliffs of the St. Lawrence River.

The generals in charge of both armies were highly decorated soldiers. General Louis-Joseph de Montcalm, a career soldier, commanded the French troops in the fortress. His opponent, General James Wolfe, was fresh from an inspired victory over the French at Louisbourg on Cape Breton Island, off Canada's Atlantic coast.

The armies were evenly matched with about 4,500 to 4,800 soldiers each. The French, however, had several advantages. First, they were stationed safely within the walls of the city, perched on a fifty-foot cliff overlooking the St. Lawrence River. Second, the weather favored the French, who believed that they could wait out the British. With winter approaching, threatening to ice over the river, the British would not be able to keep their ships in the water much longer. And with the British ships gone, supplies would again flow freely to the garrison at Québec. Wolfe knew he had to do something to draw Montcalm from the fortress. If he could meet the French army on an open field, he believed that his highly trained, veteran army would easily defeat the French, who were mostly militia forces.

In Wolfe's first attempt to draw the French out, he landed his troops at Point Levis, on the south bank of the St. Lawrence, opposite Québec. He began a bombardment of the fortress, hoping that it would force the French to leave. Although "most of the lower town was destroyed, Montcalm would not be drawn out."

British soldiers approach Québec, overlooking the St. Lawrence River.

Wolfe's next effort also failed to achieve the result he wanted. He landed some troops upriver of Québec, hoping that this would draw troops from the garrison. Montcalm did send out six hundred men, but only to guard the paths from the river to the fortress. With French soldiers now protecting the paths, Wolfe's men would never be able to reach the top of the cliffs.

Then British scouts returned with news. There was a small French camp at Anse-au-Foulon, about a mile and a half west of the city. With this intelligence, Wolfe believed that he could now use a deception strategy sometimes called "uproar east, attack west" to lure the French into a battle that would be their undoing.

He ordered Admiral Charles Saunders to move the British fleet to a position opposite one of Montcalm's main camps east of the city. The fleet needed to give the impression that it was preparing for an attack. Montcalm fell for the demonstration deception, moving troops to guard against a British assault from that point in the river.

In the meantime, Wolfe launched his main action. He sent a small "band of eager volunteers" ashore near Anse-au-Foulon and eliminated the soldiers encamped there. Now one of the roads to the heights near Québec was open, and Wolfe brought as many troops as possible up it. Before long, he found the open field he had been hoping for: a farmer's field just west of Québec that would become known as the Plains of Abraham. In the early morning, he deployed 3,300 regular soldiers in two lines that stretched across the field for a little more than half a mile. His instructions to his men were emphatic: do not fire until the French are within forty paces. This time the French did come. Alerted by a French soldier who had escaped the assault at the camp, Montcalm marched his troops to face the British on the Plains of Abraham. As one historian wrote, "It was a time to defend not to attack. . . . But Montcalm did exactly what Wolfe wanted." He put his undisciplined soldiers against the professional soldiers of King George.

The British held their fire as the French approached. Wolfe had ordered his men to charge their muskets with two balls each in preparation for the engagement. Some of the French soldiers fired random shots. Then the British line launched a withering volley, instantly cutting down many of the French soldiers. The British soldiers stepped forward a few paces before unleashing another deadly volley at the stunned enemy. The British pressed on, firing as they advanced. More French fell. The army was "disintegrating, falling back in disorder into the town." Wolfe's success came at a high price: both he and Montcalm were mortally wounded in the battle. Wolfe died on the battlefield; Montcalm died in Québec that night.

The fall of Québec was the turning point in the French and Indian War, and it was Wolfe's deception that gave the British the opportunity they needed to defeat the French. One historian calls it "one of the most momentous battles in world history" because it drove the French from the territory that was to become Canada and "produced the political circumstances in which the United States of America emerged."

A little more than a century after the Battle of Québec, the United States was beset by the American Civil War. Deception played a role in many of the war's battles, with individual field generals devising and implementing deception operations. Neither the Union nor the Confederate army had any central agency that created deceptions and passed them to the commanders to use. While both sides engaged in deception, Confederate generals did so more often. This isn't surprising, considering that the Confederate army had fewer resources than the Union army and so needed deception to level the battlefield.

The acknowledged master of deception for the Confederate forces was General Thomas Jonathan "Stonewall" Jackson, who told his officers, "Always mystify, mislead, and surprise the enemy." Jackson's time as a commander was short, as he was accidentally shot by one of his own men on May 2, 1863, during the Battle of Chancellorsville, and died soon afterward. But in the few years that he commanded Confederate troops, his style of warfare had an undeniable impact.

TWO IMPORTANT new forms of communication used in the Civil War were flag signaling and the telegraph. Both were innovative and useful, but neither was secure. With the introduction of the telegraph, messages could now easily be sent across miles. However, these messages could just as easily be intercepted and read by the other side. Flag signaling, also called wig-wag signaling or aerial telegraphy, involved the use of flags between two and six feet square, which could be seen at a distance—again a handy method, but one that was visible to friend and foe alike.

In order to secure information sent during wartime, both sides needed a way to encode their messages, a cipher system. In the simplest cipher system, each letter of the alphabet is replaced by a single letter, number, or symbol. For example, the letters might each be assigned a number, where A = 1, B = 2, C = 3, and so on to Z = 26.

The wig-wag system used by the Union army was developed by Albert James Myer, an assistant U.S. Army surgeon. The story goes that while serving in New Mexico in the 1850s, Myer got the idea for his signal system by "watching Comanches making signals with their lances to other groups of Indians on adjacent hills." (One of the officers who assisted him in developing his system was Lieutenant Edward Porter Alexander, who defected to the Confederate army at the start

Right: Myer's cipher wheel, used by Union soldiers to send secret messages

of the war and was responsible for much of the early Confederate signaling.) Myer's system involved waving a flag (or a torch, for nighttime transmissions) to the left, right, or center; between movements it was returned to an overhead position. The letter *B*, for instance, would be sent by moving the signal flag in these steps: overhead, right, overhead, right, overhead, right, overhead, right, overhead.

To encode messages sent by flag signaling, Myer used a cipher disk, a device originally developed by the Italian architect Leon Battista Alberti in the fifteenth century. A cipher disk is composed of two movable wheels, an outer wheel about five inches in diameter and an inner wheel about four and a half inches wide.

The inner wheel shows letters of the alphabet in a random order that is the same among individual wheels. The outer

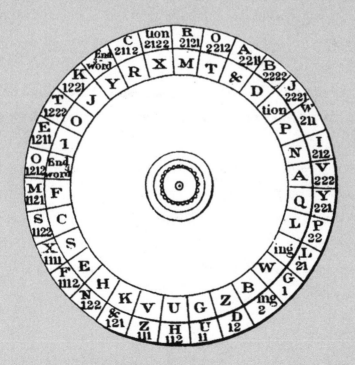

wheel contains another random alphabet, each letter accompanied by a number. This number indicates how the signalman would move his flag for the letter. The flag movement for *D*, for example, is indicated by the number 12, meaning left-right. The signalman signs the letters of the outer wheel, and his recipient "translates" them using the letters on the inner wheel.

For the disk to work, both sender and receiver need to know the key for setting the inner wheel. The key might be as simple as setting the *A* on the inner wheel to a letter that changes daily, according to a predetermined key word. For example, the key word might be *VISIBLE*, meaning that on the first day, the inner *A* is matched with the outer *V*, as in the illustration. As you can see, the *Z* is lined up with *D*, *V* with *Z*, *S* with *X*, and so on. The next day, the inner wheel is turned so that *I*—the second letter in the key word—lines up with *A*. Since this is a shift of one place, all the outer letters would shift one place. The key would continue to change until all of its seven letters had been used.

To encipher its messages, the Confederate signal corps relied on the Vigenère cipher, another Italian invention, in this case dating from the sixteenth century. As with the cipher disk, a key is needed to use the Vigenère cipher to create a coded message. A soldier might, for example, use HELP as a key to send the message CANNOT DEPART. The message would be printed without spaces between words. The key, HELP, is then written under it, until each letter in the message has a letter in the key beneath it.

	A	B	C	D	E	F	G	H	I	J	K	L	M	N	O	P	Q	R	S	T	U	V	W	X	Y	Z
A	A	B	C	D	E	F	G	H	I	J	K	L	M	N	O	P	Q	R	S	T	U	V	W	X	Y	Z
B	B	C	D	E	F	G	H	I	J	K	L	M	N	O	P	Q	R	S	T	U	V	W	X	Y	Z	A
C	C	D	E	F	G	H	I	J	K	L	M	N	O	P	Q	R	S	T	U	V	W	X	Y	Z	A	B
D	D	E	F	G	H	I	J	K	L	M	N	O	P	Q	R	S	T	U	V	W	X	Y	Z	A	B	C
E	E	F	G	H	I	J	K	L	M	N	O	P	Q	R	S	T	U	V	W	X	Y	Z	A	B	C	D
F	F	G	H	I	J	K	L	M	N	O	P	Q	R	S	T	U	V	W	X	Y	Z	A	B	C	D	E
G	G	H	I	J	K	L	M	N	O	P	Q	R	S	T	U	V	W	X	Y	Z	A	B	C	D	E	F
H	H	I	J	K	L	M	N	O	P	Q	R	S	T	U	V	W	X	Y	Z	A	B	C	D	E	F	G
I	I	J	K	L	M	N	O	P	Q	R	S	T	U	V	W	X	Y	Z	A	B	C	D	E	F	G	H
J	J	K	L	M	N	O	P	Q	R	S	T	U	V	W	X	Y	Z	A	B	C	D	E	F	G	H	I
K	K	L	M	N	O	P	Q	R	S	T	U	V	W	X	Y	Z	A	B	C	D	E	F	G	H	I	J
L	L	M	N	O	P	Q	R	S	T	U	V	W	X	Y	Z	A	B	C	D	E	F	G	H	I	J	K
M	M	N	O	P	Q	R	S	T	U	V	W	X	Y	Z	A	B	C	D	E	F	G	H	I	J	K	L
N	N	O	P	Q	R	S	T	U	V	W	X	Y	Z	A	B	C	D	E	F	G	H	I	J	K	L	M
O	O	P	Q	R	S	T	U	V	W	X	Y	Z	A	B	C	D	E	F	G	H	I	J	K	L	M	N
P	P	Q	R	S	T	U	V	W	X	Y	Z	A	B	C	D	E	F	G	H	I	J	K	L	M	N	O
Q	Q	R	S	T	U	V	W	X	Y	Z	A	B	C	D	E	F	G	H	I	J	K	L	M	N	O	P
R	R	S	T	U	V	W	X	Y	Z	A	B	C	D	E	F	G	H	I	J	K	L	M	N	O	P	Q
S	S	T	U	V	W	X	Y	Z	A	B	C	D	E	F	G	H	I	J	K	L	M	N	O	P	Q	R
T	T	U	V	W	X	Y	Z	A	B	C	D	E	F	G	H	I	J	K	L	M	N	O	P	Q	R	S
U	U	V	W	X	Y	Z	A	B	C	D	E	F	G	H	I	J	K	L	M	N	O	P	Q	R	S	T
V	V	W	X	Y	Z	A	B	C	D	E	F	G	H	I	J	K	L	M	N	O	P	Q	R	S	T	U
W	W	X	Y	Z	A	B	C	D	E	F	G	H	I	J	K	L	M	N	O	P	Q	R	S	T	U	V
X	X	Y	Z	A	B	C	D	E	F	G	H	I	J	K	L	M	N	O	P	Q	R	S	T	U	V	W
Y	Y	Z	A	B	C	D	E	F	G	H	I	J	K	L	M	N	O	P	Q	R	S	T	U	V	W	X
Z	Z	A	B	C	D	E	F	G	H	I	J	K	L	M	N	O	P	Q	R	S	T	U	V	W	X	Y

CANNOTDEPART

HELPHELPHELP

The next step is to find the C at the top of the Vigenère square (shown above) and then find the H (from HELP) along the left edge of the square. The first letter of the code is at the intersection of the C column and the H row, which means that the letter J would be the first letter of the secret message. By repeating that process for the rest of the letters, a secure message would be created. A would be written as E, N would be written as Y, and so on.

Both of these cipher systems relied on a key, which was good for security but had its downside. The key needed to be changed frequently—and always kept from the enemy's hands.

Above: Vigenère square used by the Confederate army to send secret messages

The deception that typifies Stonewall Jackson's mind-set occurred in June 1862, when he "marched and counter-marched his little Confederacy army in a bewildering choreography" in the Shenandoah Valley of Virginia in an attempt to confuse and confound the Union army. It was at a time when the war hung in the balance for the Confederacy. General George B. McClellan was ready to lead his Union soldiers to deliver a deathblow to the capital of the Confederacy, Richmond, Virginia, where most of the Confederate troops were encamped. McClellan was expecting reinforcements in the form of separate forces led by General Irvin McDowell and Major General Nathaniel Banks. If these two armies could meet up with McClellan's troops, they would engage in a pincer movement against Richmond, and all would be lost for the Confederacy.

Before that could happen, General Robert E. Lee concocted a deception that would keep Banks's troops close to Washington until Stonewall Jackson's army could race to Richmond to reinforce the soldiers defending the capital. Lee, always ready to exploit the weakness of the enemy, knew that he needed to convince the Union army that an attack on Washington, D.C., was being planned. Jackson's job was to make sure that Union commanders continued to fear that the Confederacy planned to fight its way into Washington.

Jackson performed his work admirably. He and his men raced up and down the Shenandoah Valley, "striking where

General Stonewall Jackson, Confederate master of deception

least expected and disappearing again, leaving four different Union commanders wondering what had hit them." As
Jackson closed in on Washington, he had to maintain the
deception that Washington would be next on his list of victo-
ries. President Abraham Lincoln and Secretary of War Edwin

Stanton, "still somewhat apprehensive" over Washington's security, decided that McDowell's troops needed to remain in Washington. As Stanton wrote to McClellan, "You will give no order . . . which can put [McDowell] out of position to cover this city."

One of the reasons Jackson's deceptions were so successful is that he insisted on the strictest security when he was about to engage in a deception. He would often not even tell his officers what he was planning. When they complained, he answered, "If I can deceive my own friends, I can make certain of deceiving the enemy." To that end, Jackson spread rumors that the army was indeed heading to the Potomac. He ordered his engineers to draw up a map of the valley, a sign that he was planning to remain in the area. All his men were ordered to answer "I don't know" if questioned by anyone about their order of battle. And to make the attack on Washington seem even more certain, Lee released federal prisoners, due for parole, allowing them, as one historian noted, to "see the westward movement of Confederate forces. The Union troops could count the regiments and learn of their destinations."

The deception exceeded Lee's expectations. Jackson escaped a trap set for him in the Shenandoah Valley, defeating Major General John C. Fremont at Cross Keys, Virginia, and Brigadier General James Shields at Port Republic, Virginia. Jackson and his army then rushed to Richmond to reinforce

Lee's army for the Seven Days' Battles that were to follow. The Confederacy survived for two more years.

Following the surrender of General Lee in Appomattox, Virginia, in the spring of 1865, the United States enjoyed a period of about forty years in which, other than the brief Spanish-American War in 1898, it was not involved in a war. With the nation at peace, there was no motivation for the military to continue to develop tools of deception.

CHAPTER 2

CAMOUFLAGE AND HAVERSACKS

In earlier wars, such as the American Revolutionary War and the Civil War, deception was generally the brainchild of a single person, usually the battlefield commander, who had to implement covert operations in the heat of combat. But World War I, "the war to end all wars," brought a clear shift in the role of deception by the military. Deception tactics and strategies became institutionalized and played a larger part in planning. In England, decisions about deception were made by the War Office in London, and its efforts to use camouflage became one of the first organized attempts at deception in battle. The British military grew to be particularly adept and avid users of camouflage. In a sense, they wrote the early version of the "book" on deception, although they did get a bit of help from their French allies.

By December 1915, World War I had been raging for more than a year, and the United States was still more than a year away from joining the Allies to fight the Central Powers. The British War Office arranged for painter Solomon J. Solomon to sail to France to learn what a group known as the *camoufleurs* was doing and to determine if the British army should create its own camouflage unit.

At Amiens, France, Solomon found a group of artists who were "working out the right colors for disguising and screening and also making realistic dummies, including armored trees for use as observation posts." French observation posts near the front lines could be used to direct British artillery strikes; in order to be most effective, they needed to be as close to the front as possible—and so needed to be well concealed. General H. E. Burstall, commander of Canadian artillery, asked Solomon if he could aid the French efforts by designing and making forward observation posts—OPs, also called Oh Pips—disguised as trees. Solomon accepted the challenge and returned to England to work with a team of "sappers," or combat engineers.

Solomon's trees were made of oval steel cylinders, constructed in two-foot sections. They were just wide enough for a man to work his way up inside the structure to a folding seat near the top. From there, ten to fifteen feet above the ground, he could observe every activity through holes or slits. While the basic design was suitable, Solomon knew that in order to be properly concealed, the Oh Pips needed bark to make them look more like real trees.

Solomon decided that a good source of bark was the forest around King George's royal estate at Windsor Castle, so he wrote to the king for permission to take bark from a decayed willow tree. "Secrecy in the affair," he wrote, "is of the highest importance." He was correct, of course, in believing that it was better to ask the king for the bark rather than to trust the discretion of a private citizen. The king's secretary replied from Buckingham Palace that "the King will be glad to give you every facility you require either at Windsor or at Sandringham." With the help of two scene painters and a theatrical prop maker, Solomon fashioned tree cover that would pass for real bark when viewed from a distance. He sewed chunks and strips of bark to sheets of canvas that would then be wrapped around the trees' steel shell.

On March 15, 1916, the first tree was erected. Solomon's trees and other versions of the camouflage tree saw action on the battlefields of Europe, where they served their purpose well. A 1917 issue of *Popular Mechanics* featured a picture of a steel tree, noting that "a structure of this sort standing amid tree trunks that have long survived artillery fire is almost sure to escape detection by the enemy." Another version found in Belgium was nearly eighteen feet tall, with "'lumps' on the outer shell, made of chicken wire and grass like materials to resemble either burls or lumps of moss or lichen. . . . The 'bark' . . . appears to include crushed sea shells to give it a rough texture." Regardless of the construction of these steel trees, their purpose was the same: deceiving one's enemies to gain an advantage over them.

With the Oh Pips designed, the British *camoufleurs'* work was only beginning. On January 18, 1916, Solomon and his team—a draftsman, a scene painter, a property man from a theater, and a master carpenter—sailed to France and set up shop in Amiens. They spent a week studying what their French counterparts had done and then got to work.

Solomon was not content with merely creating camouflaged Oh Pips. He saw other ways that camouflage could be improved to deceive the Germans and their allies. One area that the painter felt needed attention was the covering that protected the trenches. It was common to use mackintosh sheets, a waterproof covering similar to a tarp, over the trenches. But the sheets collected pools of water, making them unwieldy and heavy. And, looking at them with the eyes of a painter, Solomon thought that the pattern painted on the sheets was too smooth and didn't match the surrounding terrain.

A model of an observation post used in World War I

CAMOUFLAGE IN NATURE

IT SHOULD COME as no surprise that a partnership between visual artists and the military led to some groundbreaking uses of camouflage in war. Artists, after all, study the ways in which colors interact, and landscape painters in particular are attuned to the nuances of color in nature. This knowledge has been put to effective use by the military in order to protect personnel and equipment and to support deception strategies.

Although the ancient Greeks wrote about animal camouflage, it became more of an area of study after Charles Darwin wrote about it in his 1859 book, *On the Origin of Species*. He noted the role of camouflage in the evolution of some animal species, saying that those species that did not develop camouflage tactics were less likely to survive and reproduce and, therefore, more likely to become extinct. Since Darwin's time, other zoologists have studied animal camouflage and come to a better understanding of how it works.

There are two main types of animal camouflage: crypsis (from the Greek word for "hidden"), when an animal is hard to see because of its ability to match its background, and mimesis (from the Greek for "imitation"), when an animal masquerades as something to which a predator is indifferent. Mimesis isn't limited to appearance but can also include sounds, behavior, and even scent.

For many animals, crypsis, or blending in, is the most effective form of camouflage. The coloration of many woodland creatures—deer, beavers, and woodchucks, for example—blends with the colors of trees, plants, and ground of the woods. The colors of sea creatures—such as dolphins and sharks—blend with the blues and grays of their underwater environment. Many arctic and subarctic mammals and birds even change their coloring for different seasons. The rock ptarmigan, a bird in the grouse family, has white winter plumage but sports a mottled brown in the summer, and the snowshoe hare has a white coat in winter but a brown one when the snow melts.

In another type of crypsis, called countershading, some animals' coloration is darker on their upper side than on their underside. The top of a swimming penguin, for example, is dark, making it difficult to spot from above because it blends in with the dark water. Its lower side is light, making it hard to spot from below because it blends with the sky above. Military *camoufleurs* adopted this form of camouflage for airplanes, painting the tops of planes in patches of green and brown to blend in with the ground when viewed from above, and the bottoms white, blue, or gray so that, when viewed from below, they blend into the clouds and sky.

Another crypsis trick is to eliminate shadows, which are often a giveaway to predators. Some desert lizards, for example, hide from predators by flattening their bodies into the ground and freezing, eliminating their shadow and making them blend in smoothly with their environment. World War I military *camoufleurs* used the principle of shadows, but in reverse: by *adding* shadows to dummy equipment, set up to make their forces appear larger or to mislead the enemy as to their placement. Painting shadows on the ground, for example, could make a flat, fake plane look three-dimensional from the air.

Mimesis, the camouflage technique of imitating another creature or object, is often used by potential prey animals to

An owl blends in with the bark of a tree.

avoid being eaten. The peppered moth caterpillar masquerades as a twig, and some grasshoppers look like dry leaves. But some predators use mimesis to lure their prey. Flower mantises, for example, look, as their name suggests, like flowers. Pollinator insects land on them—only to be snagged by the mantis for lunch.

This form of animal camouflage has been used by armies and navies, starting with the British Royal Navy in World War I. Q-ships—also called special service ships or mystery ships— were small freighters or old trawlers that were loaded with hidden guns in a collapsible deck structure. They were deployed with the mission of luring German U-boats to come close enough to be sunk by the hidden guns. At the peak of their use, the British had a fleet of 366 Q-ships, which were responsible for sinking nearly a dozen U-boats. However, once the secret was out, the Q-ships' effectiveness dropped off sharply.

From blending in to luring prey, nature has given a plethora of ideas to visual artists in their work as *camoufleurs*.

As an alternative, Solomon tried using string to make a "cat's cradle" that he envisioned could be covered with leaves and branches, making a more lifelike camouflage. His prop man took over and in short order wove a square yard of netting. Solomon was the first to implement the use of fishing nets instead of canvas as a camouflage for trenches—as well for guns, supplies, and ammunition stores.

While most deceptions in war, like camouflage, are designed to help a side win a battle and advance an army's objectives, there are also ample instances when an army needs to pull off a deception in order to minimize a potentially catastrophic toll on the battlefield. A classic example of such a motivation occurred during World War I, in 1915, when the British were mired in the disastrous campaign at Gallipoli, a peninsula to the north of the Dardanelles, a strip of water between Greece and Turkey. It was only a well-executed deception that kept the loss of life at Gallipoli from being even worse. As historian Alan Moorehead put it in his book *Gallipoli,* "everything that was done with stealth and imagination was a success, while everything that was done by means of headlong frontal attack was foredoomed to failure."

By the end of 1914, the war's combatants were locked in a deadly standoff. The western front extended from Switzerland to the English Channel. Trench warfare was brutal. Conditions were primitive and barbaric. The troops lived in cramped quarters and often suffered from body lice, diarrhea, and dysentery. Their diet was poor: mostly canned beef, army biscuits, and jam, without fresh fruit or vegetables. Weather conditions were extreme: broiling sun in the summer carried the stench of death, while the winter brought rain, snow, and bone-chilling temperatures.

In a war that would see more than 8.5 million men killed in battle, 21 million injured, and nearly 8 million prisoners of war and missing in action, 1914 was only the beginning. Yet the British and French were already feeling the political heat to break the impasse, to deal a devastating blow to the Central Powers, which included the German Empire, the Austro-Hungarian Empire, the Ottoman Empire, and, from 1915 on, the kingdom of Bulgaria. The main players of the Allies, or Entente Powers, were France, the United Kingdom, Russia, Italy, and (beginning in 1917) the United States.

The Allies, led by the British, decided to open another front in the east. This move was designed both to distract the public from the deadly stalemate on the western front and to give the Allies a chance for a victory. Strategically, it would give the Allies an eastern base from which to launch an attack on the Central Powers. The British and French were pushing to capture Constantinople (modern-day Istanbul), the capital of the Ottoman Empire. It was hoped that the capture of this strategic Middle Eastern city would also induce the Ottoman Turks to end their part in the war.

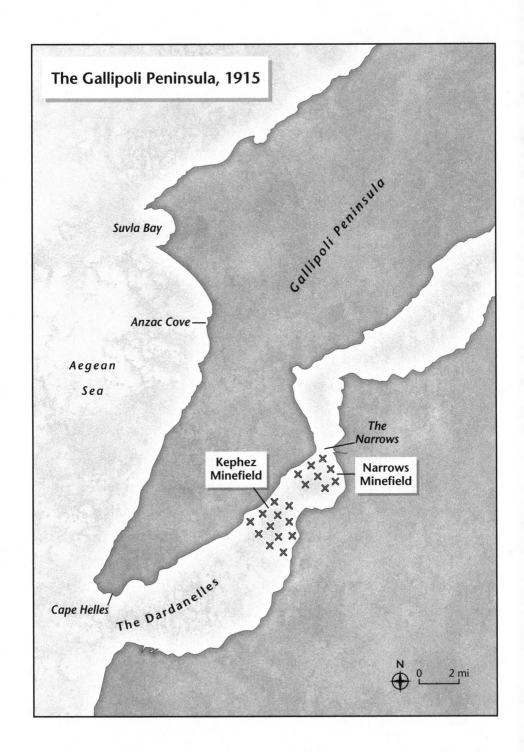

The Gallipoli Peninsula, 1915

Suvla Bay

Gallipoli Peninsula

Anzac Cove

Aegean
Sea

The
Narrows

Kephez
Minefield

Narrows
Minefield

Cape Helles

The Dardanelles

N
0   2 mi

However, the greatest reason to capture Constantinople was that it would allow the Allies to control a water supply route to their Russian ally. A land route was blocked by Germany and Austria-Hungary. Other water routes posed their own difficulties. The White Sea was too far to travel from England and clogged by ice for much of the year. The Germans controlled the Baltic Sea, which left the Black Sea as a point of attack. But the Black Sea was accessible only through the Bosporus, a strait that forms part of the border between Europe and Asia. Before British and French warships could get through the Bosporus, they had to pass through the Dardanelles, a very narrow body of water, which squeezes at one point to only about a mile and a quarter wide. As the Allies were to learn, the geography of the Dardanelles would make it an easy position for the Turks to defend.

The discussion on how to attack Constantinople soon turned to matters of military strategy between those who wanted a strictly naval approach and those who wanted to land troops at Gallipoli. At the strong insistence of Winston Churchill, First Lord of the Admiralty (later, during World War II, England's prime minister), the naval option was accepted. Despite Churchill's enthusiasm, the plan was doomed from the start because it was based in part on intelligence that underestimated the size and location of the Turkish troops.

The attack began on February 19, 1915, with British and French warships pounding the Ottoman artillery positions on

Gallipoli. The initial success of the bombardment pushed the Turks back from their first line of defense and led Churchill to believe that the ships would make it to Constantinople in two weeks. The Turks had other ideas. Rather than trying to match firepower with the British and French warships, they trained their mobile field guns and howitzers on the minefields that they had strung across the narrow passage. When the Allied ships hit the mines, the vessels were disabled or destroyed, and the Turks fired away at them. Unless the British could clear the minefields, they couldn't advance. But when they sent in minesweeping ships, they were hammered by the Turkish howitzers. The Allies could not overcome the Turks' strategic position. The minesweepers sent out to clear the mines never completed the operation. In the end, four Allied warships were sunk, three more severely damaged by mines or enemy fire, and seven hundred sailors lost their lives.

The Allies could no longer sustain an attack relying solely on naval forces. They regrouped and decided that they would put troops ashore on the beaches on the west side of the Gallipoli peninsula. The problem was that the troops were not immediately available. It took six weeks to amass the necessary personnel, many coming from the Australian and New Zealand Army Corps (ANZAC) with little battlefield experience. In the meantime, the Turks and the Germans fortified Gallipoli, building roads and moving troops across the Dardanelles. The beaches where the British Empire's troops would come ashore were strung with barbed wire. More mines were slipped into the water. The Turks were ready for an Allied invasion.

The Allied troops stormed ashore on April 25, 1915, in an attempt to establish two beachheads on Gallipoli: one at Cape Helles, on the southernmost tip of the peninsula, and the other at Gaba Tepe, some twelve miles up the western coast. The name of the small cove near this landing site was soon changed to Anzac Cove, to honor the ANZAC soldiers who formed the bulk of the invasion force. While the Allied troops were able to establish the two beachheads, it came at great loss of life, and the Turks still held the high ground at the top of cliffs overlooking the beaches, keeping the Allied troops from advancing.

The Allies sent more troops ashore in August, this time at Suvla Bay, farther up the coast from Anzac Cove. Their plan was to join up with the troops in the other two locations and sweep across the peninsula. However, none of the armies could extricate themselves from the beachheads where they were pinned down. The Allied troops dug trenches, preparing for the long haul. The situation in Gallipoli began to remind the military commanders and politicians uncomfortably of the stalemate on the western front.

The casualties in Gallipoli mounted as the campaign dragged on. Casualties for both sides—including killed and wounded—neared nine hundred thousand by the end of the debacle, or about half of the total Allied forces deployed

there, and 60 percent of the Turks. With casualties mounting from battle, disease, and the extreme weather conditions,
the Allied leadership needed to face the truth that continued
fighting would only lead to more casualties, not to mention
disgrace on the world stage.

The possibility of an evacuation reared its ugly head
and was first considered on October 11, 1915. There was
resistance. Sir Ian Hamilton, commander of the U.K.'s
Mediterranean Expeditionary Force, opposed the plan. Many
in the government and the military could not accept the
notion of retreat and defeat. That was the path of the weak. To
complicate matters for the British, they had opened a second
eastern front in Greece, and they received news that Bulgaria
had entered the war as an ally of the Central Powers. Bulgaria
now provided a land route by which Germany could easily
resupply the Ottoman soldiers. No more British troops could
be spared to send to Gallipoli to turn the tide of the battle.
England had no choice: the government decided to evacuate
all 150,000 soldiers remaining on the peninsula.

Those who opposed the evacuation warned that it could
not be accomplished without severe additional casualties.
Hamilton stated in anger that "casualties of such an evacuation would run at up to 50 percent." However, others believed
the number of casualties would be considerably lower. A
successful evacuation could be achieved only by deception. Incredibly, the possibility of evacuation was publicly
debated by two members of Parliament — a breach of security

that would normally doom a deception, but in this case it had the opposite effect. Turkish and German agents were convinced that such a public and heated debate was surely a clever plan to get them to lower their guard and commit troops to foil the evacuation. Such a move, they reasoned, would weaken their defenses on other parts of Gallipoli. Although the British had not planned the leak as a deception tactic, they could not have hoped for a better response to this unintended mistake.

Hamilton was replaced as commander by General Sir Charles Munro, who favored the evacuation plan. He came to the conclusion that "our chances of success were infinitely more probable if we made no departure of any kind from the normal life we were following. A feint which did not fulfill its purpose would have been worse than useless." The evacuation plan was built on a complex schedule that orchestrated the movement of tens of thousands of troops. Brundell White, chief of staff to the ANZAC commander, devised the "bold plan [that] involved spiriting men, animals, and equipment away at night while not allowing the Turks to glimpse or even guess that they faced a progressively weaker force." If there was genius in the evacuation plan—referred by some as a "silent night withdrawal"—it was in that deception technique: demonstrating that the Allied troops were carrying on business as usual.

The plan had three phases. The initial phase of the evacuation involved moving troops and supplies that would be consistent with a typical winter campaign, lulling the enemy at a time when armies were frequently satisfied to maintain their positions, rather than engage in aggressive offensive tactics. The second stage of the evacuation would continue to reduce the number of troops and leave just enough to fend off a Turkish attack for about a week. The final stage would move the last twenty-five thousand troops over the nights of December 18 and 19.

But no matter how good the evacuation plan was, it meant little if it could not be executed with a minimum of casualties. This called for a deception plan that would mask the intentions of the British troops. The cornerstone of such a deception was creating a convincing demonstration that would fool the Turks into believing that life in the British encampments at Suvla Bay and Anzac Cove was continuing as normal as Christmas approached. The Turks observed the soldiers coming and going, moving supplies on mules. What the Turks didn't know was that they had fallen for a British substitution tactic. The Turks were seeing the same men every day, and the crates that they were moving were empty. Under the cover of darkness during a ten-day period, eighty-three thousand Allied troops moved from their trenches to Williams Pier at North Beach, which was between the two camps. The beleaguered soldiers walked down to the piers and boarded transport ships that took them to safety.

One of the deception tactics that the British troops used

were "silent stunts," which were periods of time when they fired no guns at the Turks, who became accustomed to such lulls and perhaps, as one historian suggested, felt that "a live and let live policy was being adopted." Then, when a stunt had run its course, a few shots were fired at random times, something else that the Turks came to expect. Other soldiers acted out scenes to further the notion that the Allied troops were at ease with the winter calm. One group was ordered to hang around on what was called Artillery Road, so that the Turks could see them enjoying a leisurely smoke. A cricket match was staged on the Shell Green. All these deceptions had one goal: to let the Turks see that life was proceeding normally at the camps. Yet every night, thousands of troops were safely evacuated under their noses.

The soldiers moved under cover of darkness, marching down from the mountains to the pier. Supplies and equipment were handled by the Indian Mule Cart Corps, who moved their animals quietly without the notice of the Turks on Sniper's Nest. As one soldier later wrote, "How silently these mules behaved. They had big loads, but they were perfectly quiet . . . except for a slight jingle of a chain now and then. . . . I doubt if at 1,000 yards [the Turks] could see them at all—possibly just a black serpentine streak."

Fortunately, the officers on Gallipoli showed a higher regard for security of the deception than the members of Parliament had. In fact, many troops had no idea that an evacuation was going on until the second week of the deception. Clearly, the officers knew the importance of revealing information only on a need-to-know basis.

One part of the deception involved a "drip rifle," a device that was designed by a soldier, William C. Scurry, to fool the Turks into thinking that shots were being fired by soldiers in the trenches. The drip rifle was a clever device that worked on a simple principle. Two gasoline cans were placed one above the other. The upper can contained water.

A drip rifle at a British camp at Anzac Cove

The bottom can was empty, but rigged with a string that was attached to the trigger of a rifle. As the last of the soldiers left a trench, they would punch a small hole in the bottom of the upper can. Water then dripped from that can into the lower can. When enough water entered the lower can, the tension on the string ultimately pulled the trigger. By putting varying amounts of water into each can, rifles fired at random times from the Allied trenches—without any soldiers present.

Some accounts of the drip gun give its importance legendary stature, claiming it played a large role in the success of the evacuation. However, one historian debunked that notion, writing that of "all the many legends of Anzac, that of the drip gun was the most exaggerated." He found that "very few drip guns" were set up, and they each fired but a single shot. Such random shots may have given the evacuating soldiers an additional hour or so to make their way to the waiting ships at Williams Pier.

By December 20, about eighty-three thousand troops had slipped away from Suvla Bay and Anzac Cove. A small force remained on Cape Helles to maintain a British presence in the Middle East. Within a week, the British government reconsidered this and "successfully evacuated the remaining 35,000 troops, 4,000 animals and 1,000 tons of stores from Helles." By the middle of the night on January 9, 1916, all of the Allied troops had left Gallipoli.

In the last days of the evacuation, the final ten thousand

men continued activities to convince the Turks that life in the British trenches was normal. Then, in midafternoon, they began a feint attack at Helles to distract the Turks' attention from the evacuation. At dusk, the final fifteen hundred troops trudged through the trenches and made their way to the ships

Evacuation of Allied troops and supplies from Gallipoli

waiting at the pier. One of the last soldiers to leave Gallipoli wrote that, as he walked through the trenches, his footsteps on the frozen ground "echoed right through the trench, down the gully . . . and you could hear this echo running ahead. Talk about empty, I didn't see a soul. . . . It was a lonely feeling."

One of the final tasks that the troops performed before evacuation was the destruction of as much of their stores as possible to keep supplies from the hands of the Turks. The Allies ripped open sandbags, spoiled flour and fuel, and fouled engines in remaining equipment. Finally, they "set off the charges under a mountain of oil-soaked kit: volcanic explosions mushroomed flames into the night sky, rained debris on the last boats leaving, and started, too late, a terrific firework show of enemy shooting and shelling." Although many supplies were destroyed, the Turks still found, according to historian Nicholas Rankin, "more useful material than you can shake a stick at. It took two years to ship it all to Istanbul."

The deception was complete. The evacuation was a success with only a few minor injuries. Nonetheless, most historians agree with A. J. P. Taylor, who called the evacuation of Gallipoli "the successful end of a sad adventure." German intelligence, embarrassed by the deception that had covered the evacuation of nearly one hundred fifty thousand troops, was certain that the Turks had been bribed to allow the evacuation. Such was not the case, but the Allies did little to counter that rumor, believing that the less the Germans knew about their deception tactics, the better. They also liked the notion that there was some distrust between two of the Central Powers.

• • •

After the debacle on Gallipoli, the British were searching for a success on the battlefield that would boost morale on the home front. Perhaps they would have some good news in the Middle East, where hostilities had spread from western Europe through the Balkans and had reached as far as Egypt and Palestine.

The British feared that the Turks would now attack the Suez Canal, which the British controlled. Connecting the Mediterranean Sea to the Red Sea, the canal provided the quickest water route between Europe and India and other British colonies in the Pacific. The British would never allow that trade and supply route to be threatened.

As a force of twenty-five thousand Turkish soldiers began the 180-mile march across the desert from Beersheba to the Suez Canal on January 14, 1915, the British were ready to defend the canal, adding thirty thousand Indian soldiers to the Suez defense. Three weeks later, the Turks began their attack. The Indian soldiers, reinforced by Australian infantry, beat back the Turks. The Turks were "heavily reliant upon total surprise for any possibility of success, [but] the British were nevertheless warned of impending attack by reconnaissance aircraft." After losing two thousand soldiers (to the British 150), the Turks retreated to Beersheba. However, the victory "led to pressure from the British government . . . to invade [Turkish]-controlled Palestine."

The British army was stalled in its march from Egypt

to Jerusalem by strong and well-trained German and Ottoman troops. Late in June 1917, command of the Egyptian Expeditionary Force (EEF) was given to General Sir Edmund Allenby, a "soldier of great vigour and imagination, who was able to create a personal bond with his troops." Allenby was known to his men "(with both fear and affection) as 'the Bull.'" And British prime minister David Lloyd George was counting on the Bull to change the progress of the EEF and defeat the German and Turkish forces at three spots:

- the walled city of Gaza on the coast of the Mediterranean Sea
- Beersheba, thirty miles to the east and one of the primary supplies of water in the desert of Palestine, with artesian wells that had been rigged with explosive charges by the Germans
- Jerusalem

Twice, British and ANZAC troops had suffered severe casualties in their assaults of Gaza. Morale in the U.K. had dropped. The British war cabinet was "close to desperation." The country needed a victory on the battlefield in Palestine. The prime minister left no room for doubt about what he expected from Allenby when he sent him a three-word message: "Jerusalem. By Christmas."

But what was Allenby to do? He couldn't get to Jerusalem without dislodging the Turkish and German troops in Gaza.

And his predecessor had been beaten back twice when British forces tried to take the walled city with frontal attacks. Perhaps he could expect help from the Royal Navy off the coast in the Mediterranean. But one of the rules of thumb for an attacking army is that it must always outnumber the defenders. Any way he counted them, Allenby's troops did not.

Allenby considered his options and decided that he would create a deception that would lead the Central Powers to believe that he was attacking Gaza, when his real target was Beersheba. With the momentum of a victory (and the water) at Beersheba, Allenby could swing to the west and take Gaza, then move northeast to Jerusalem. If he could get the enemy to believe that his primary objective was Gaza, the Central Powers would move no troops to reinforce Beersheba, Allenby's true objective.

To draw the Germans and Turks into their bluff, the British used a strategy that became a classic deception practice: the haversack ruse. This ruse relied on the Germans and Turks believing that secret intelligence had fallen into their hands because of a mistake by the British. (The British would use the same strategy in World War II in Operation MINCEMEAT.) In this case, the mistake would be the dropping of a haversack (a canvas bag with a long strap that allowed it to be hung across the shoulders) in the desert to be picked up by a Turkish patrol. The sack would be filled with misleading documents, along with other items designed to convince the enemy that the documents were genuine.

The haversack ruse was part of an overall deception operation created by Brigadier General Sir Philip Chetwode, Allenby's commanding officer. The haversack ruse itself was the brainchild of James D. Belgrave, a twenty-one-year-old lieutenant colonel who proposed its use, including detailed suggestions of what to include in the sack, in a long-secret memo to Allenby.

To make the ruse seem more convincing, Allenby wrote to headquarters in Cairo asking for assistance—troops, air support, field artillery—and leaked the request to German and Turkish intelligence operatives. He knew that such assistance simply wasn't available, but he wanted to create the illusion that he didn't have enough troops or equipment to wage a successful Palestine campaign.

One morning in early October 1917, a British intelligence officer, believed to be A. C. B. Neate, rode out into the desert toward the village of el Girheir, northwest of Beersheba, where he was certain to encounter Turkish troops. But that was part of his plan. He *wanted* to be noticed. Turkish scouts, as expected, gave chase, but soon lost interest in the solitary rider. Neate dismounted and fired a couple of shots at the Turks, not really caring if his aim was true. The Turks renewed the chase, this time firing at the British intelligence officer as he rode.

At a safe distance, Neate began the charade that was part

of his plan. He slumped in the saddle, dropped his rifle, then slid to the sand. He appeared to have been wounded by the Turkish shots. He staggered around, making a feeble attempt to gather some items that had fallen to the ground. Then he hurriedly pulled himself back into the saddle, "accidentally" dropping his haversack, canteen, and binoculars before racing off again, hunched in the posture of a wounded soldier. He outdistanced the Turks and made it back to camp safely.

The Turks quickly recovered the haversack that he left behind. They found it filled with items of interest that had been carefully created to fool them: "all sorts of nonsense about [British] plans and difficulties." The sack contained a number of documents, some official, others personal. All the items created a sense of authenticity: a twenty-pound Bank of England note, a "tidy sum in those days—to give the impression that the loss was not intentional"; a handwritten letter from an English woman to her husband, chatting about their baby, whom he had not seen; a letter from a resentful officer complaining about the foolishness of the British plans; information about a British code system that would allow the Turkish and German intelligence staff to decode British wireless communications; and, the most important pieces of the haversack ruse, orders and a notebook commonly used by the British staff officers.

An agenda for a staff meeting suggested that the British would mount a two-part operation in the desert. The first part would be a feint attack on Beersheba, a diversion from the major attack of Gaza. In addition, the notes indicated that the attack on Gaza would take place in November (some weeks after the date of the real attack).

Knowing that the haversack, once discovered by the Turks, would be rushed to German intelligence agents for analysis, the British wanted to add more credibility to the deception. The enemy needed to be convinced that the material in the haversack was legitimate. So, the day after the haversack was dropped, the British ordered a scouting party to search for it near the front.

To authenticate the fake code that was in the haversack, the British used it to send low-level intelligence about the offensive against Gaza. They also sent an encoded message that General Allenby would be visiting Cairo until November 7, leading the Germans to believe that any attack would not happen before that date. Finally, they sent a message stating that Neate needed to report to General Headquarters to face an investigation into the "lost secret papers."

Apparently, the deception operation worked because the German commander, Major General Friedrich Kress von Kressenstein, remained convinced that the British would attack Gaza yet again. He refused to move any troops to reinforce Beersheba. He readied his troops for an attack on the fortress city from the desert and from the Mediterranean.

In the meantime, the British had an order of battle for their two attacks. The XXI Corps would feign an attack on Gaza, making as much noise as possible while, at the same time, limiting the number of casualties. The surprise attack on Beersheba would be led by General Harry Chauvel, an Australian, and his Desert Mounted Corps. On October 30, as Gaza fell under an artillery barrage from "218 guns . . . to fool the Turks into believing that a full frontal attack was imminent," forty thousand British troops slipped through the desert, double-timing the thirty miles to Beersheba, arriving for a daylight surprise attack. The success of this march was, in part, made possible by the presence of planes from Royal Flying Corps and the Royal Naval Air Service that constantly patrolled the skies above Gaza. These British aircraft prevented Germans from flying and observing the huge troop movement to the east.

British soldiers inspect a tank demolished near Gaza.

The march itself was remarkable because, despite the constant and deafening noise of the bombardment of Gaza that obliterated other noise, it was still extremely difficult to quietly move tens of thousands of troops and animals. The troops needed to "muffle the thud of hoof beats, the creak of leather, the snort of horses, and the bang of metal gear."

The attack on Beersheba was an astounding success of "heroic magnitude." The Desert Mounted Corps easily penetrated the first ring of defense around Beersheba. The Turkish commander then made a series of errors that would doom him and the precious water that he was to protect. As he looked out over the desert, he saw no large mass of British infantry that was close enough to worry him. What he didn't know was that Allenby and Chauvel were not infantry officers. They were cavalry officers, leading thousands of troops on horseback, troops that could cover ground at an astonishing clip. And they did, quickly overpowering the Turkish troops at Beersheba with such "a spectacular charge" that the Turk commander did not have the time or the men to detonate the explosives set in the wells.

With victory assured, the British troops drank deeply from the wells that they had conquered. But, in about a week, they returned to the road, this time riding toward Gaza, a city that continued to get pounded by British heavy guns. In less than a day of fighting, the city fell and the German and Turkish troops, shocked by the defeat, abandoned Gaza and retreated in disarray into desert north of the city. But the

British army had one more conquest before it could claim its final objective. Chauvel's battle-tested Desert Mounted Corps pushed on to Jerusalem, entering the city on December 10, 1917, two weeks before the Christmas deadline imposed on Allenby by Prime Minister Lloyd George, who considered Jerusalem a "Christmas present for the British nation."

Luckily for the British, the Germans appear to have fallen for the leaked information, the fake coded messages, and the bogus documents in the haversack because they did not stop to think that if this plan—a feint to attack Beersheba when the real target was Gaza—was a fake, then the real plan was the opposite, that is, that the Gaza attack was the diversion for the real attack on Beersheba. Had they shifted reinforcements to Beersheba and awaited the British forces, the outcome of the whole campaign could have been different. But they remained convinced that the British would attack Gaza. The early bombardment added to that conviction. As a result, they made no substantial change in the number of troops at each city, which, in a sense, weakened both. Neither Beersheba nor Gaza could withstand the ferocious attack of the Desert Mounted Corps and the other troops. In a matter of days, the Germans had lost the Palestine desert.

CHAPTER 3

OPERATION BERTRAM

In the decade after the end of World War I, Europe tried to get back on its feet, but it wasn't easy. As the 1920s came to a close, the Great Depression took hold of the United States and Europe, turning the economic prosperity of the postwar years on its head. Millions of workers lost their jobs. In Europe, families struggled to rebuild their lives on war-wrecked land without the many who had been killed. Such desperate times were the perfect breeding ground for the seeds of discontent that were planted by Adolf Hitler in Germany. He promised a cultural and national renewal for Germany, which had been devastated and humiliated by the war and by the subsequent peace settlement at Versailles. Appointed chancellor (head of government) of Germany in 1933, Hitler hurtled down the road to another war by invading Poland on September 1, 1939.

Two days later, England, France, Australia, and New Zealand declared war on Germany. At the end of 1941, the United States declared war on Japan, Germany, and Italy, and Hitler declared war on the United States.

By 1940, the British were fighting the Axis powers in North Africa. Not only was the war in Africa a test for the fighting forces of England and its allies; it was also an opportunity for the British to dust off and refine some of the deception tactics they had developed in World War I. In fact, many of the ingenious deception schemes that the Allies used so successfully later in World War II were born in the desert of North Africa in the early months of the war. With their enemies in control of the northern part of the continent, the Allies sought any advantage to stop the Axis troops from Germany and Italy, especially the movement of the famed Afrika Korps, a massive expeditionary force of German troops and tanks led by Field Marshal Erwin Rommel, the legendary "Desert Fox."

In his rise as a battlefield commander, Rommel utilized effective deception techniques — which the Allies were quick to adopt and use against him. In 1941, for example, Rommel paraded his tank division into Tripoli, Libya, knowing that the world would be watching. He had to present a formidable show of force. German tanks roared down the main boulevard past the reviewing stand with local and Nazi officials watching. It was an impressive sight. Who knew that the Nazis had so many tanks? The truth is: they didn't. Rommel had pulled a simple deception on the onlookers. When a tank moved beyond public view, they turned the corner and circled back, passing the reviewing stand again . . . and again. In all, the same division of tanks passed the gathered officials four times.

From the western part of the North African desert, the Germans and Italians wanted to sweep east to reach the Nile River and control the Suez Canal, putting a choke hold on the supply route so vital to the Allies in Egypt. The British needed to prevent this from happening. And so they turned to a handful of elementary deceptions.

In one of their initial successes, the British forces used deception to surprise a much larger Italian and Libyan army that had marched to a position about sixty miles west of Cairo. Sir Henry Maitland "Jumbo" Wilson, commander in chief of British troops in Egypt, knew that because of the many spies lurking in Cairo, he had to maintain strict security of the looming British offensive. To maintain the secrecy of the operation, Wilson even kept his own troops in the dark about the real intention of their mission, telling them that they were part of a massive training exercise. And Wilson did more than that as well. He created dummy headquarters to simulate notional (fake) units. He issued false orders to support his cover story. And to convince spies that the troop buildup was nothing more than a training exercise, he remained in Cairo, separated from his troops, until December 9, 1940, the day of the attack. The Italians were fooled by the attack and within days their army crumbled, allowing the British to take one hundred thirty thousand prisoners, twelve hundred pieces of artillery, and four hundred tanks.

General Archibald Wavell, commander in chief of British troops in the Middle East, recognized the value of such deception and gave his full support to more deception operations, believing that the "practice of deception in the Desert was developed into an art" by his countrymen. He approved the formation of a special unit at General Headquarters (GHQ) in Cairo, tasked with developing subterfuge and counter-intelligence strategies in the desert. Commanding the unit was Colonel Dudley Clarke, beginning his role as the master-mind of deception operations.

In April 1941, Clarke's deception unit was officially recognized with a cover story that it was part of GHQ. But the unit still needed a name. "Advanced Headquarters Airborne Force" was suggested, but rejected as being too obvious for a deception operation. "Avd HQ 'A' Force" was finally accepted. The name was "deliberately vague . . . could stand for anything," which pleased Clarke. And so the "A" Force was born.

The "A" Force began earning respect in early 1941, when Clarke used the Royal Air Force to drop flares, explosives, and decoy parachutes within sight of the Italian troops holding the Siwi Oasis, southwest of Cairo. The Italians, certain from all the pyrotechnics that they were outnumbered, hastily pulled out of the Siwi and retreated west.

While Clarke was in London and Washington working on cover plans for Operation TORCH, a British-U.S. invasion of French North Africa launched in November 1942, he also created the deception plan that would support the operation. The "A" Force's successes were mounting—they had, for instance, recently contributed to Operation CRUSADE, which resulted in an Allied victory over the German army in Egypt and Libya. And Wavell trusted them to derail Rommel's Afrika Korps.

Despite this success, the Germans were still a potent threat in North Africa. The war was not going well for the Allies, especially in western Europe, where the Nazi war machine rolled on relentlessly through Poland, Belgium, the Netherlands, Austria, and France. Winston Churchill was intent on gaining ground in North Africa. He had replaced his commander in chief, Claude Auchinleck, with General Bernard Law Montgomery. Monty, as he was commonly called, was said to be "as quick as a ferret and about as likable." The new commander in chief agreed that the Allies needed to hold the desert near El Alamein, a city about 150 miles west of Cairo, no matter the cost. The Desert Fox had to be defeated before his troops could get any closer to Cairo.

THE PRACTICE of naming secret operations originated during World War I, with Germans operations on the western front. The names they selected were borrowed from religious, medieval, and mythological sources: Archangel, Roland, Mars, Achilles. The U.S. Army began using code names for deception operations for security reasons during World War II.

Early U.S. code names reflected color-coding of secret missions. The operation to send reinforcements to Iceland, for example, was dubbed Operation INDIGO, while plans to occupy the Azores, a group of Atlantic islands about nine hundred miles west of Portugal, was called Operation GRAY. And later, Gold was the code name for one of the landing spots during the Normandy landings.

As U.S. war efforts became more active and varied, color names were no longer sufficient for naming operations. In early 1943, the War Plans Division "culled words from an unabridged dictionary to come up with a list of 10,000 common nouns and adjectives that were not suggestive of operational activities." They avoided tip-off words like proper nouns, geographical terms, and names of ships.

The system Hitler used for naming his secret operations often disregarded such cautions, sometimes with results that were detrimental to his war efforts. His operation to invade

Russia was originally called FRITZ, to honor the son of the plan's creator, Lieutenant Colonel Bernhard Von Lossberg. However, Hitler would not allow his massive operation to have such a common name. Wanting a name that would reflect the grand scale of his invasion, he changed the name to BARBAROSSA, the folk name of the twelfth-century Holy Roman emperor and folk hero who extended Germany's borders. Although the name was considered inspirational to many Germans, the Führer was fortunate that the Russians didn't get hold of the name of the secret operation and make the historical connection between the name and twelfth-century German expansions.

Hitler wasn't as lucky when he chose the name of Operation SEALION for his plans to invade England. British agents not only learned the name of the operation, but they were also able to make the connection between the name and Hitler's objective. That intelligence was one of the reasons the British were able to win the Battle of Britain and end Hitler's plans to claim British soil.

According to military historian Gregory C. Sieminski, Winston Churchill was "fascinated with code names and personally selected them for all major operations." In fact, at one point in the war he insisted on "personally approving every operation name before it was carried out." In 1943, he sent a memo to field commanders that contained his guidelines for naming operations. He warned against "well-sounding names which do not suggest the character of the operation," saying that he wanted to be certain that no mother was told "her son was killed in an operation called 'Bunnyhug' or 'Ballyhoo.'" It was Churchill who named the Normandy invasion Operation OVERLORD.

Operation JERICHO: U.S. bombers blast Amiens Prison, in France, in an attempt to free French Resistance prisoners.

Despite all its security efforts, British intelligence had a scare in the months leading up to D-day when one morning the crossword puzzle of the *Daily Telegraph* contained the code names of the invasion beaches—Juno, Gold, Sword, Utah, and Omaha—as well as the name of the whole operation. Intelligence agents swooped down to investigate the puzzle maker. They concluded that the puzzle maker—a country schoolmaster—knew nothing of the impending invasion of France. His choice of words for his puzzle was merely a bizarre coincidence. But forty years later, a student of the puzzle maker claimed that his teacher had "inserted the words in the puzzle after hearing American soldiers talk about the invasion."

Throughout World War II, the U.S. military continued to use code names that were meaningless as a way to safeguard operational security until General Douglas MacArthur changed the naming practice in one significant way, allowing code names to be declassified and released to the press once the operations were under way. Thus began the practice of assigning names for their public relations value. It was an opportunity to boost morale in the field and at home with operation names like THUNDERBOLT, ROUNDUP, KILLER, RIPPER, COURAGEOUS, AUDACIOUS, and DAUNTLESS.

When the United States entered the Korean War, the Defense Department once again created colorful names for military and humanitarian operations. Among the five hundred names created were: BIG STICK, a plan to destroy the Communist supply complex and regain the city of Kaesong; BLUE-HEARTS, a draft plan for an amphibious landing that became CHROMITE, the landing at Inchon; CLAM-UP, an operation to fool the Communists by imposing silence along the front lines, February 10–15, 1952; KILLER, a U.S. offensive to the Som River; SCATTER, a screening plan for the repatriation of prisoners of war; STRANGLE, an air operation to disrupt North

Korean logistics by strategic bombing of its railroad system; and TALONS, a ground offensive to bolster the Eighth Army's eastern position.

During the Vietnam War, operations were given nicknames that were descriptive of the missions. BLASTOUT, for example, described a joint U.S.–South Vietnam operation designed to increase the area of control around the base at Da Nang, and the slowly intensifying strategic bombing effort that began shortly after BLASTOUT was called ROLLING THUNDER.

After the end of the war in Vietnam, the Joint Chiefs of Staff created a computer database to "fully automate the maintenance and reconciliation of nicknames, code words, and exercise terms." The Code Word, Nickname, and Exercise Term System—NICKA, for short—is still in operation. It is not, however, a random word generator for nicknames. Rather, it is, as historian Sieminski notes, "merely an automated means for submitting, validating, and storing" code names. Of course, the "actual code names used by the military are only a single word long and are classified as top secret."

The practice of creating code names for public consumption continued in the first Gulf War. When U.S. troops arrived in the Middle East after Iraq invaded Kuwait, their mission was to protect Saudi Arabia, so the mission was called DESERT SHIELD. However, when the mission became an offensive mission to drive the Iraqis from Kuwait, the name of the mission was changed to DESERT STORM. Realizing that the desert theme resonated with the American public, the Pentagon used it in other operations as well: DESERT SABER, for a ground offensive; DESERT FAREWELL, for the redeployment of American units after the war; and DESERT SHARE, for the distribution of surplus food from military units to the poor in the U.S.

When the U.S. invaded Iraq following the terrorist attacks against the U.S. on September 11, 2001, the initial operation was given the upbeat name IRAQI FREEDOM. Nearly ten years later, when the mission was focused on efforts to stabilize the country, the name was changed to Operation NEW DAWN.

The German front line ran for about thirty-five miles from the Mediterranean Sea near El Alamein south to the Qattara Depression, a 7,500-square-mile basin of sand dunes and salt marshes that would be impassable for military movement. The Allies decided to attack the northern end of the front with a massive assault force. However, they schemed to convince the Germans that the attack would be aimed at the *southern* end of the front. If Rommel fell for this false order of battle, he would keep half of his tank corps in the south, leaving the north vulnerable. The British knew that it was going to take a massive deception campaign to give the Allies under Monty the edge they needed to destroy the Afrika Korps. Otherwise, a battle in the desert could well become a last stand for the British in North Africa.

An out-and-out surprise attack would be foolish; the open terrain of the desert would not permit it. No, the Allied command needed to deceive the Nazis, to get them to act upon what they *thought* they saw, to act in a way that would play into the hands of Allied forces. The "A" Force would be put to the test to create and execute such a crucial deception involving coordinated efforts by many military units.

The "A" Force's plan, code-named BERTRAM, began in Cairo with lies—or, as it is known in the intelligence community, misinformation. The basic story that was skillfully leaked centered on the fiction that the British could not begin any serious offensive activity in the desert until winter. They needed time, the story claimed, to "assess long-range prospects in the Northern front." Further rumors hinted that the British had their sights set on Crete, an island off the southern tip of Greece, and would mount only a minor desert offensive, feigning to attack the northern end of the German front in Africa before slamming the southern end with the bulk of their troops. The misinformation even included a specific date for this southern attack: the moonless night of November 6. The Americans' heavy Sherman tanks that the British were counting on would not be available any earlier.

With this bogus story circulating, the British Embassy made a show of scheduling many social events for late October, including parties and cruises on the Nile. Important British generals booked rooms at one of Cairo's most luxurious hotels. A fake conference was organized in Tehran, Iran, for October 26, and all the British field commanders were scheduled to attend. To help disseminate these lies, embassy officials were a little "careless" in letting such details reach the ears of known German informants.

Finally, the Allies used what they called their Black Code to give legitimacy to all the rumors of activity. Early in the war, the Americans had developed what they believed to be a secure code, dubbed the Black Code, for secret transmissions. But they soon discovered that the Germans had acquired the codebook and were using it to read Allied secret messages. How had the Germans gotten their hands on the codebook? A British investigation revealed that an Italian office worker with lock-picking skills had broken into the U.S. Embassy in Rome, photographed the book, and handed it over to the Nazis.

The first impulse of the British intelligence officers was to stop using the Black Code. However, after further consideration, they decided to create a new secure code system, but to continue using the Black Code to feed false information to the Abwehr, Germany's military intelligence organization. Judging from the intercepts at Bletchley Park, the British code-breaking headquarters, the Abwehr never realized that the Allies had turned the pilfered code to their own advantage.

With misinformation spread and rumors circulating, the first stage of the deception was complete. The seeds had been planted. The "A" Force waited, counting on the Nazis to react in a way that would draw them deeper into the deceptions of Operation BERTRAM.

The success of Bertram rested on convincing the Nazis that Operation Lightfoot, at the southern end of the front, was a major Allied offensive. British forces needed Rommel to keep half of his one thousand tanks there to repel an attack. Further, the Germans had to divert other valuable equipment and resources away from the location where the real attack would be launched. If Rommel kept his tanks in the south for just four days, that would give the Allies enough time to smash through the northern front and drive the Nazis farther into the desert to the west.

The real attack date was set for two weeks earlier than

the leaked date of November 6. British forces would move on October 23, a night with a full moon. The Allies, meanwhile, led by the "A" Force, needed to create a fake show of force in the south while hiding the true buildup of personnel, supplies, and equipment being relocated toward the north. They needed to disguise five thousand tons of stores in the north while showing a fake six thousand tons in the south. In all, perhaps one hundred fifty thousand men and ten thousand vehicles had to be relocated across an empty plain without the Desert Fox's knowledge. As Anthony Cave Brown noted in his book *Bodyguard of Lies,* everything had to be "concealed and revealed according to a plan that required the artifices of a master conjurer."

Monty's chief of staff laid out the stakes when he told Clarke: "Well, there it is. You must conceal 150,000 men with a thousand guns and a thousand tanks on a plain as flat and as hard as a billiard table, and the Germans must not know anything about it, although they will be watching every movement, listening to every noise, charting every track. [Every low life] will be watching you and telling the Germans what you are doing for the price of a packet of tea. You can't do it, of course, but you've bloody well got to!"

The "A" Force had a strong faith in substitution as a deception technique. If the enemy is accustomed to seeing something—such as a ten-ton truck or a supply dump—after a while, he will lose interest in it and no longer give it careful scrutiny. So, the Allies established three storage areas east of the front. Code-named Murrayfield North, Murrayfield South, and Melting Pot, these facilities held armored equipment such as tanks and self-propelled guns. The Nazis knew of these stores—the Allies made no attempt to hide them—but were comfortable with them, as long as the numbers didn't grow. What was important to the Allies was getting the Nazis to see that the equipment didn't move toward the front lines.

Once these storage areas were established, the British moved the equipment under cover of dark to Martello, a staging area much closer to the Allies' real point of attack. Why didn't the Nazis notice the armored equipment moving

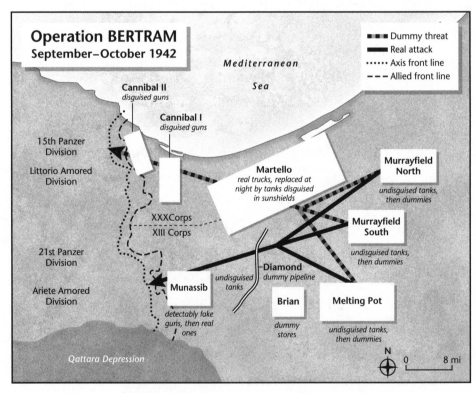

Battle map for Operation BERTRAM

closer to the front? Because the Allied camouflage experts disguised the tanks as less threatening ten-ton trucks by placing a framework known as a sunshield over them. And each piece of fighting equipment that rumbled to Martello was replaced in the storage area by a constructed or inflatable dummy. In all, these operations involved four thousand real vehicles, as well as 450 dummies and seven hundred sunshields. So, from the Nazis' point of view, everything remained the same.

At the same time that the armored equipment was moving, the Allies established Brian, a dummy depot for food and ammunition, stacks and piles of empty crates, and cans resembling supplies. Brian reinforced the idea that the southern end of the front was the real point of attack. Finally, the armored equipment moved once again, still closer to the northern point of attack, once again camouflaged as heavy trucks. Also in place were artillery pieces that were camouflaged to look like three-ton trucks. Not far from the artillery was a fuel dump that was skillfully concealed from any air reconnaissance.

Is it possible to hide massive military equipment in the desert? The "A" Force proved that it could be done. As one historian noted, "A supply dump could be made to look like a lorry [truck], a lorry to look like a tank, and a tank can hide itself inside an apparent supply dump." Large pieces of artillery were moved back to back, then covered with "cannibals"—coverings made of hessian, a burlap-like fabric—that made them look from the air like "thin-skinned" three-ton trucks.

Ammunition was also hidden in a unique way. Boxes of ammo were laid out in an irregular pattern, but only one box high. The boxes were then covered with hessian and sand, and, from the air, were indistinguishable from the surrounding desert.

Perhaps some of the most ingenious work by the "A" Force was the design and construction of dummy tanks and other vehicles. Fake vehicles were built of panels woven from the fronds of palm trees. The Allies hired local workers to weave thousands of these panels. Once the palm panels were fashioned into the shapes of tanks, they were covered with camouflage nets and gave the impression of a large armored force, "apparently camouflaged and awaiting the movement orders, probably to the south."

A further touch to convince the Nazis was a fake water pipeline heading south, code-named Diamond. A pipeline already existed from El Imayid to Alam el Khadim, a distance of about twenty miles. But the Allies, wanting to signal to the Nazis that the British would need lots of water for the troops that would be part of the southern attack, built a dummy pipeline that extended twenty-five miles farther south.

The Allies didn't rush the construction of their fake pipeline. The engineers and soldiers working on it—actually using four-gallon fuel cans—moved at a pace that would have the work completed just in time for November 6. However,

Members of the "A" Force conceal a tank to make it look like a supply truck.

the Nazis did not realize that at nightfall, the fake pipeline placed that day was dug up, the trench filled in, and the same cans used each day, giving the appearance that the pipeline construction was progressing on schedule. To complete the charade, three dummy pump houses were built, as well as overhead tanks and stations to fill cans with water. Nazi spy flights over the construction could not tell that the construction trucks parked near the site were dummies. To make the whole scene seem more true to life, the Allies went so far as to divert traffic around the pipeline.

The "A" Force leaders knew that Operation LIGHTFOOT—the diversionary attack in the south—needed to be convincing. If the Nazis were not duped by it, the real attack, in the north, would be doomed. Brian and Diamond would help, but the Allies wanted to do more. They hoped that another deception, at a spot called the Munassib Depression, would add to the illusion. This scheme placed dummy artillery batteries in a position that appeared to be in support of LIGHTFOOT. However, the deceivers intentionally did nothing to maintain the dummy artillery. Even the nets covering the "guns" were allowed to rot. Once the Nazis saw this, they were quick to believe that the big guns were fake and posed no threat to them. As the date of attack drew closer, the Allies executed a masterful double bluff, replacing the dummy artillery with real guns that they would use in the southern diversion attack.

Yet another Allied operation hid six thousand tons of

stores about five miles from the northern attack point, not far from El Alamein. Crates of supplies were stacked to resemble ten-ton supply trucks and covered with nets. Leftover supplies were stacked near the "trucks" to give the appearance from the air that they were part of temporary camps.

In addition, the British needed to hide fuel near the northern battle site, but without blasting out a storage crater. Such activity five miles from the front would surely attract the Nazis' attention. Lieutenant Colonel Geoffrey Barkas, a film set designer, and Major Tony Ayrton, a visual artist and Barkas's assistant, noticed a number of unused drainage trenches lined with masonry tiles. Ayrton, with his painter's eye, noted that the color of the masonry tiles was similar to the color of the British fuel cans. Why not, he suggested, line the trenches with the thousands of fuel cans and see if they would blend in with the tiles and, therefore, be invisible from the air?

He experimented with one of the trenches, lining it with cans. Then he flew over the trench and photographed it. When he returned and looked at the photographs, he discovered that he had been right. Because of the colors of the cans and shadows, he could not discern any difference between the trenches with masonry tiles and the one with cans of fuel. The British began moving the cans of fuel to the trenches. Over three nights, cans with two thousand tons of fuel were laid in the trenches, hiding in plain sight. Once again, the Nazis were fooled by the magicians of the "A"

Force. Subsequent intercepted German messages indicated that their recon flights had noticed nothing different about the trenches.

With all the pieces finally in place, the decisive battle of El Alamein (officially known as the Second Battle of El Alamein) began on Friday, October 23, 1942, with a tremendous artillery bombardment of the German trenches, part of the LIGHTFOOT deception operation. Because of minefields laid by the Germans near El Alamein—in a no-man's-land called the Devil's Gardens—the progress of the Allied tanks was limited. The danger and difficulty of clearing mines for the tanks allowed only a path wide enough for a single-file column. But when one tank was damaged in that narrow corridor, it blocked the others behind it, making them easy targets for German artillery. By nightfall, Monty had to concede that his tanks and troops had not gotten as far as planned.

Two days later, facing limited success in the south, Monty pulled some of those units and turned to the north, beginning Operation SUPERCHARGE. Churchill was furious, feeling that the victory the Allies had spent months constructing was slipping away. What he didn't know was that Rommel's forces had been severely damaged in the LIGHTFOOT attacks. The Allies had three times as many tanks as his remaining three hundred. To Churchill's astonishment, Rommel quickly moved what was left of his Afrika Korps north to the Mediterranean, convinced that that was where the next Allied point of attack would be. There he encountered an Australian army that fought ferociously. One historian noted that even Rommel commented on the "rivers of blood" in the region.

British Crusader tanks in the African desert

Rommel pitted "tank against tank," but soon admitted that his troops were hopelessly outnumbered. Germany couldn't allocate additional resources to Africa. Hitler ordered Rommel to continue regardless, but Rommel refused. He would sacrifice no more of his soldiers. As more and more Allied tanks joined the battle across the German perimeter early in November, Rommel ordered his beleaguered troops to retreat to the west. British troops pushed onward, capturing the Axis base of Tel el Aqqaqir, which effectively ended the battle of El Alamein. The campaign claimed the lives of about thirty thousand Axis troops and about thirteen thousand Allied troops.

While the deception operations at El Alamein by and large worked as planned, historians agree that Rommel's defeat was sealed by the lack of supplies and reinforcements. Rommel had begged Hitler for fuel and other goods; the Allies knew of his desperation from intercepts at Bletchley Park. They also knew of the German tankers that were steaming across the Mediterranean, only to be sunk by Allied bombs.

Whatever the causes, Winston Churchill got the victory he needed so badly. He appeared before the House of Commons and declared, "The Battle of Egypt must be regarded as an historic British victory." Some historians call it a turning point of the war. With a victory in Africa, Allied forces had a base from which they could drive across the Mediterranean, capture Sicily, and fight their way up the boot of Italy to attack what Churchill called "the underbelly of the Axis."

But El Alamein was a turning point in another significant way as well. The deceptions of the "A" Force were successful. Captured German documents revealed that Nazi commanders never realized that they were being fooled by Operations BERTRAM and LIGHTFOOT. Victory at El Alamein "put the final seal of approval on deception" as a part of future battle plans. And it served as a template for what would become the greatest deception of the war, Operation BODYGUARD.

CHAPTER 4

OPERATION BODYGUARD

By December 1943, the war in Europe had been grinding on for four years. The armies of the Third Reich had gobbled up most of the continent, in a war that "was claiming 10 million people a year." Despite some setbacks in Russia, Italy, and North Africa, the Nazis were still a formidable foe. Nearly a million German soldiers formed a sixteen-hundred-mile Atlantic Wall, a "line of fortification that was the strongest in history save the Great Wall of China." The future of Europe would depend on the success of an Allied invasion of western Europe. But how could the Allies expect to breach that wall and take the battle to the Nazis?

While the Allies pondered a plan to invade Europe, Winston Churchill came to the realization that there was only one way that an invasion would have any chance of success:

Europe
June 6, 1944

Axis-dominated areas
Areas under Allied control
Neutral countries

Barents
Sea

Norwegian
Sea

FINLAND

NORWAY

North
Sea

SWEDEN

ESTONIA

UNITED KINGDOM

DENMARK

LATVIA

IRELAND

LITHUANIA

EAST
PRUSSIA

U.S.S.R.

NETHERLANDS

POLAND
(General
Government)

Atlantic
Ocean

GREATER
GERMANY

BELGIUM

EASTERN
POLAND

LUXEMBOURG

BOHEMIA
MORAVIA

UKRAINE

FRANCE

SLOVAKIA

SWITZERLAND

AUSTRIA

HUNGARY

ROMANIA

PORTUGAL

ITALY

YUGOSLAVIA

Black
Sea

SPAIN

BULGARIA

SPANISH MOROCCO

ALBANIA

GREECE

TURKEY

FRENCH
MOROCCO

TUNISIA

Mediterranean
Sea

ALGERIA

N

0   300 mi

LIBYA

EGYPT

At the time of the D-day invasion, Germany controlled nearly all of Europe.

deception. Somehow, the Allies had to fool the Germans about the location and date of the invasion. As everyone understood, if the invasion failed, any chance of stopping Hitler would be lost.

Even though Hitler had a firm grip on Europe, the Allies knew that he was vulnerable. He needed to defend the entire west coast of Europe against an invasion that he *knew* was coming. Hitler didn't know exactly where or when the invading army would come ashore, but, according to historian Ben McIntyre, he believed that "if the invaders could be successfully resisted in the early stages of the assault, even for one day, then the attack would fail." He decided to maintain his two large army groups where they were—the Seventh Army in Normandy, the Fifteenth up the coast at Pas-de-Calais—and count on either army to move quickly to the point of invasion. Without knowing it, he was actually playing into the hands of the Allies by spreading his troops over such a wide area.

Such was the situation one morning in December 1943, when General Sir Stewart Menzies, chief of the British Secret Intelligence Service (MI6), and Colonel David Bruce, chief of the American Office of Strategic Services (OSS), the predecessor of the CIA, walked to Churchill's secure London bunker and presented Plan JAEL, a blueprint for a deception operation that would dupe Hitler and his Abwehr.

Colonel John Henry Bevan, head of the London Controlling Section (LCS), a secret agency that was the brainchild of Churchill, had prepared a draft of Plan JAEL in the summer of 1943, naming it after a heroine in the Bible who used deception to kill an oppressor of the Israelites. In Bevan's original plan, the Allies would not invade Europe for another year, focusing instead on an attack of the Balkans to the east and on an intense aerial bombardment of Germany, which was code-named Plan POINTBLANK.

Churchill, Roosevelt, and Stalin meet at Yalta.

Bevan had presented his plan to the Allied high command, whose reaction was less than enthusiastic. The Allied leaders—Churchill, Franklin Roosevelt, and Joseph Stalin—met twice in November to consider JAEL. Early in December, Bevan received their revised proposal and returned to London to work on the next draft of the deception plan.

To have any chance of success, the greatest of invasions needed to be supported by the most detailed and devious of deceptions. At the center of JAEL was Churchill himself. As Colonel Sir Ronald Evelyn Leslie Wingate later wrote, it was Churchill who had "all the ideas. It was his drive, his brilliant imagination, and his technical knowledge that initiated all these ideas and plans." Plan JAEL was "intended to provide the novel experience and sinister touches" for Operation NEPTUNE, the code name for the amphibious invasion of France.

The December meeting was no more than a formality to approve JAEL, which had been agreed upon by the three Allied leaders the previous month at a meeting in Tehran. At that meeting Churchill uttered a sentence that has been quoted many times since and established something of a theme for all deception plans to follow in the war. "In war-time," Churchill said, "truth is so precious that she should always be attended by a bodyguard of lies." And, indeed, before the meeting approving JAEL adjourned, the group decided that the code name of the deception plan would be changed from JAEL to Operation BODYGUARD.

CHURCHILL COULD CONCENTRATE on planning BODYGUARD because the Royal Air Force had defeated the Luftwaffe (Germany's air force) in the Battle of Britain in 1940, greatly reducing the possibility of aerial reconnaissance of Allied troop movements by German planes. And the success of the RAF against the Luftwaffe relied on radar.

Radar is an acronym for *radio detecting and ranging.* Christian Hülsmeyer's early version of radar, which he called a remote object viewing device, was designed to prevent collisions of ships at sea. But as the war clouds appeared over Europe, scientists began to see how Hülsmeyer's invention could be used in war. Ironically, though radar was pioneered in Germany, it played a huge role in England's victory in the Battle of Britain.

In 1935, Sir Robert Watson-Watt located a plane by reflecting radio waves off its metal bulk. The discovery was crucial for the British Air Ministry, who believed that "no avenue, however seemingly fantastic," should be overlooked, including inventors who promised that they could deliver a "death ray." While no such weapon was developed, radar promised a "new and potent means of detecting the approach of hostile aircraft, one which will be independent of mist, cloud, fog, or nightfall."

The scientific principle behind radar is quite simple. Strong, short bursts of radio energy are sent into the air using a special directional antenna. When the radio signals strike an object,

they bounce back toward the point of origin, where they are converted into an electrical signal that appears on a screen. The position of the target is determined by calculating the time it takes for the radio signal to hit the target and bounce back to the antenna. Since radar uses radio waves, it can work day or night, and in all kinds of weather conditions.

In 1936, Air Ministry engineers constructed the Chain Home (CH) system along the south and east coasts of England. Its installations could identify an enemy aircraft and calculate its direction, speed, and altitude while it was fifty to sixty miles away.

Radar gave the Air Ministry the ability to move its small air resources to better defend England and provided warning time to sound air-raid sirens. It was also used to aim searchlights and antiaircraft fire, to locate enemy ships and submarines, to navigate planes, and to find bombing targets.

Above: Early radar antenna

BODYGUARD would be an Allied effort, but the main players were the British and the Americans through their intelligence and counterintelligence sections, including the British agencies MI6, responsible for espionage and intelligence matters outside of the British Isles, and MI5, the British Security Service, responsible for espionage matters on British soil, similar to how the FBI attends to domestic intelligence issues in the U.S. The United States member of the BODYGUARD deception team was the OSS, providing intelligence and special operations services. The deception operations would be run by the London Controlling Section, part of the planning staff at Churchill's headquarters. The LCS was responsible for planning and implementing deception strategies for the duration of the war.

The deception planners would rely to a large degree on special operations, a "vaguely sinister term that included a wide variety of surreptitious, sometimes murderous, always intricate operations of covert warfare designed to cloak overt military operations in secrecy." Winston Churchill was responsible for the key role that special ops played in BODYGUARD, as well as in other World War II deceptions. In fact, one historian believes that Churchill's use of special ops and the establishment of a central agency to devise and coordinate the tactics of special ops was "probably his greatest single contribution to military theory and practice." This was quite an achievement for a man whose political career was in shambles following the tragedy of Gallipoli some thirty years earlier.

A successful deception, particularly one of the magnitude of BODYGUARD, was not simply a single activity. Nor was it the work of a single agency. A deception operation of this complexity required the work of many people and cooperating agencies. After much discussion among members of the extended intelligence and military communities, the Allies settled on a strategy for BODYGUARD that would include five areas of secret activities:

- **Intelligence Gathering:** What plans was the target (Hitler) contemplating? What were Hitler's fears and insecurities? BODYGUARD had two main sources of intelligence within the Third Reich. The first, and more important, was Ultra, the code name for all intercepted secret messages sent by the German High Command and decoded by code-breakers at Bletchley Park near London. The second was the Black Orchestra, a group of German officers who were plotting the downfall of Hitler. From time to time, members of this band of traitors to the Reich passed on intelligence to the Allies.
- **Counterintelligence Activities:** The LCS took strong counterintelligence measures to make sure that Germany did not learn any details of the planned

invasion of France. Because BODYGUARD included many deception operations, a leak in any one of them could cause the whole deception to sink. To help maintain security on the operation, MI5 saw to it that any known German spies were rounded up; many were used as double agents.

- **Special Operations:** While one historian believes that special ops used in Operation BODYGUARD included only "an occasional act of thuggery," sinister measures were used more than occasionally. Such operations fell to the Special Operations Executive (SOE) behind enemy lines in France, These brave operatives found and supported resistance groups and underground organizations. Their work included sabotage, abduction, and, on occasion, murder.

- **Political Warfare:** This aspect of deception was aimed directly at non-military citizens, mostly through rumor and misinformation. It was an attempt by the LCS to lead the population to question its commitment to the policies of the Third Reich.

- **The Deception Itself:** While these five areas of the operation worked together, out-and-out deception— "the ultimate secret weapon and the most secret of all secret operations," as historian Anthony Cave Brown put it—carried the day.

All these secret activities had one ultimate goal: to deceive the Nazis about the imminent Allied invasion of Europe, to fool them about when the invading armies would come ashore and where the landing would be. It was also determined that parts of the deception needed to be maintained for at least a few days following the invasion.

BODYGUARD, then, had three main objectives. The first was to make Pas-de-Calais appear to be the place where the massive Allied attack would come ashore, when the real invasion site would be about two hundred miles south at Normandy. The second aim was to get Hitler to keep his troops at Pas-de-Calais until it was too late for him to move them to reinforce his army at Normandy. Last, BODYGUARD had to keep the actual date, time, and place of the Normandy invasion secret.

Even though the major theater for the Allied invasion would be western Europe, the Allies wanted to spread out the Nazi army as much as possible. They heeded the wisdom of Sun Tzu, who wrote in *The Art of War,* "If [my enemy] sends reinforcements everywhere, he will everywhere be weak." A successful deception can act as a "force multiplier," not by actually increasing one's personnel numbers but by giving the enemy the *impression* that one has more troops than one does. In this case, appearing to be preparing to attack in numerous places would create an illusion of higher numbers and force the opponent to prepare on all fronts.

Allied troops storm the beach at Normandy on D-day.

One of the key aspects of FORTITUDE—the major deception in BODYGUARD—was creating notional, or fictional, armies. Spreading Hitler's army along his Atlantic Wall would accomplish two things. First, the thinned Nazi army would be more vulnerable in an attack. Second, being ordered to maintain their positions, the troops would be unable to reinforce any other point of attack.

BODYGUARD included many deception operations that were meant to convince Hitler that an Allied attack could come at a number of locations. The geographic distribution of the deceptions covered the length and breadth of Europe, from Spain to Turkey. Bear in mind that Russia, the third country among the Allies, was prepared to open an attack from the east. BODYGUARD was a magnificent and intricate stained-glass window of an operation, in which the pieces needed to fit perfectly and stay in place to maintain the deception of Hitler and his intelligence officers.

Operation BODYGUARD
Subsidiary Operations

- Axis-dominated areas
- Areas under Allied control
- Neutral countries

FORTITUDE NORTH
GRAFFHAM
ROYAL FLUSH
SKYE
FORTITUDE SOUTH
QUICKSILVER
TAXABLE
IRONSIDE
GLIMMER
ROYAL FLUSH
FERDINAND
ROYAL FLUSH
ZEPPELIN

N
0   300 mi

Code Names of D-day Operations

BODYGUARD: the deception operation that would maintain the secret of the Allies' real invasion plans

FERDINAND: a plan designed to convince the Nazis that the Allies' primary landings would be from the Mediterranean, coming ashore in Italy

FORTITUDE NORTH: the cover and deception operation to convince the Nazis that the Allies were going to invade Norway

FORTITUDE SOUTH: the cover and deception operation to convince the Nazis that the Allied landings would come at Pas-de-Calais

GLIMMER: a simulated assault landing on D-day at Boulogne, near Pas-de-Calais, to keep the German troops pinned down

GRAFFHAM: an operation that convinced Sweden to support Operation FORTITUDE NORTH

IRONSIDE: a threatened attack at Bordeaux, south of Normandy, designed to keep German troops away from the actual landing site

NEPTUNE: the amphibious landings at Normandy

OVERLORD: the overall plan for the Allied invasion of Europe

QUICKSILVER: the cover and deception operation concentrating on the First United States Army Group (FUSAG) and the plan to invade Pas-de-Calais

ROYAL FLUSH: diplomatic deceptions designed to hint that some neutral nations—notably Sweden, Spain, and Turkey—were joining the Allies, or at least allowing Allied aircraft to use their airfields

SKYE: the wireless radio deception operation for the notional British-American army in Scotland getting ready to invade Norway

TAXABLE: another simulated assault landing, this one at Fécamp, northeast of Le Havre, but with the same purpose as GLIMMER and IRONSIDE: to occupy the Nazi troops and keep them away from the real landings

ZEPPELIN: the cover and deception operation directed at the Balkans and other eastern European countries under Nazi control

Despite the scope of the deceptions in BODYGUARD, the main operations were FORTITUDE NORTH and FORTITUDE SOUTH, two complicated operations that were run at the same time and designed to cover NEPTUNE.

Each of these intricate masterpieces of deception included many of the techniques that were part of earlier deceptions. But with BODYGUARD, the practices of deception in war were more organized and widespread. BODYGUARD raised the role of deception to a level never before seen in war.

CHAPTER 5

FORTITUDE NORTH

Although historian Thaddeus Holt believes that FORTI-
TUDE NORTH did not have the "life-or-death implications"
of FORTITUDE SOUTH (which masked the actual invasion of
France), it still contained plenty of moving parts that needed
to be carefully planned and skillfully executed in order for
the deception to play its part in the successful D-day invasion. The objective of FORTITUDE NORTH was to convince
the Nazis that the Allies intended to invade Norway and then
march into Germany by way of Denmark. If the Allies could
sell the Nazis on that deception, the London Controlling
Section believed that Germany would maintain its strong
presence in Norway and not move its troops to defend the
beaches of France.

The North Sea and surrounding countries, November 1943

In November 1943—seven months before the D-day invasion—the German military presence in Norway was significant: about two hundred fifty thousand soldiers, in addition to a large air force, a panzer (tank) division, and more than fifteen hundred coastal defense guns. Major Roger Hesketh, director of the section of FORTITUDE that was devoted to spreading misinformation, did the math this way: one hundred thousand troops in Norway would have been enough to "keep the native population in subjection." The rest of the German troops could be considered "an insurance against invasion."

One of the reasons that Norway presented such a good opportunity for the Allied deception units was that Hitler desperately wanted to maintain control of Norway, showing what Supreme Allied Commander General Dwight D. Eisenhower called the conqueror's mentality, a commitment to not relinquish any conquered lands. In this case, Hitler had good reason for wanting to keep Norway. The country supplied him with crucial iron ore that he needed for his war machine. He was determined to fight any threat to those critical supplies. So the Allies knew that Hitler would be quick to act on even the hint of an invasion of Norway—and the LCS planned to give Hitler all the evidence he needed to believe that such an invasion was being planned.

If the most critical operations in FORTITUDE NORTH and SOUTH were to succeed, they needed to integrate four deception techniques. There would be physical deception—specifically, the use of dummies and camouflage, as were so skillfully used at El Alamein. The second component would involve signal transmissions, releasing false information for the enemy to intercept and decipher. Messages would be multiplied to give the eavesdropping enemy the impression of more troops, located in places that would concern him.

The third technique would be "black propaganda," the

practice of appealing directly to the people of an enemy country with mostly false information, to convince them that the war isn't worth their efforts or that their leaders are lying to them. The fourth element would be the use of double agents, Germans who had been sent to England to spy for the Reich but who were turned, becoming British agents and sending mostly false information to their German handlers. One historian has noted that it is "no coincidence that for the Western Allies the biggest turning points in the war against Hitler . . . were all backed by elaborate and well-executed cover plans, which were promoted by the double agents."

Brigadier Richard Barker, a signal officer for MI5, chose Colonel Roderick MacLeod to organize FORTITUDE NORTH in Scotland. The centerpiece of his operation would be the creation of the British Fourth Army, a blend of genuine and notional (imaginary) forces. At most, the Fourth Army consisted of "only several hundred men, frantically driving around different parts of Scotland with their signals equipment," sending out "volleys of Morse code into the ether, some 350 representing a force of 100,000 men." At first, MacLeod was disappointed that he was not going to command a fighting unit in the invasion, but Barker convinced him that FORTITUDE NORTH was a crucial part of BODYGUARD. "It's terrifically important that it should be a success," Barker told MacLeod.

MacLeod began his work by choosing the man to

command the fake army that he was going to invent. The commander needed to be someone who would get the Nazis' attention with his rank and experience. MacLeod selected General Andrew "Bulgy" Thorne. MacLeod knew that Thorne was familiar to many Wehrmacht generals, who would expect him to be given only an important command.

With Thorne in place, MacLeod next set up a wireless network to fill the air with messages that could be easily deciphered by the Germans' wireless intercept section, the Y Service. The messages followed a protocol that involved all levels of the notional Fourth Army, within which corps spoke to divisions, divisions communicated with regiments, and regiments transmitted orders to battalions. In all, the fake Fourth Army consisted of one hundred thousand men divided into four infantry divisions, an airborne division, an armored brigade, and dozens of other units. The army also included its own tactical air support as well as 250 tanks and an assortment of armored combat vehicles. And almost none of it was real!

Initially, according to historian Charles Cruickshank, the "main element in the plan was the use of false radio signals to simulate existence of the Fourth Army." Getting all the elements of the radio transmission deception, code-named Operation SKYE, in order was a difficult task. First of all, MacLeod needed enough men (and the *right* men) to make the plan work.

DESPITE THE technological advances in warfare between the American Civil War and World War II, the practice of sending secret messages made few advances during that time. Whether messages were sent over landlines or as wireless radio transmissions, the basic means of sending those messages was Morse code by means of a telegraph key.

A typical telegraph key used to send and receive Morse code messages

Both sides in World War II were consistently intercepting each other's transmissions, so even when messages were encoded by something as sophisticated as the Nazi Enigma machine, they were often a weak link in military operations. It wasn't easy for Operation OVERLORD to deceive the Nazis with bogus radio transmissions.

Samuel F. B. Morse created his system of sending messages in 1830. Shortly after that, he began work on an electric telegraph. However, it wasn't until May 24, 1844, that the inventor transmitted his first message. It was sent from the chamber of the U.S. Supreme Court, in the Capitol building, and received at the railway depot in Baltimore. It stated: "What hath God wrought?" The code at that time was called American Morse code, or Railroad Morse because of its extensive use by railroads. Right before the start of World War I, an international Morse code was adopted and became the "language" for sending messages via telegraph or wireless radio.

Early Morse code receivers made small indentations (dots) and longer ones (dashes) in a paper tape that was read by a telegraph agent. However, as telegraphers became more skilled, the tapes were eliminated, and telegraph operators learned to decipher the Morse code messages by ear.

Morse code works by means of a key, a switch that turns a transmitter on or off. When the switch is held down by an operator, the transmitter is on for as long as the operator holds the switch. So, if he holds it down for half a second, the transmitter sends for half a second, which is heard on the receiving station receiver. Morse code is a combination of short and long sounds (or flashes of light) that the operators transmit and receive. This combination of *dits* (shorts) and *daas* (longs) in certain patterns

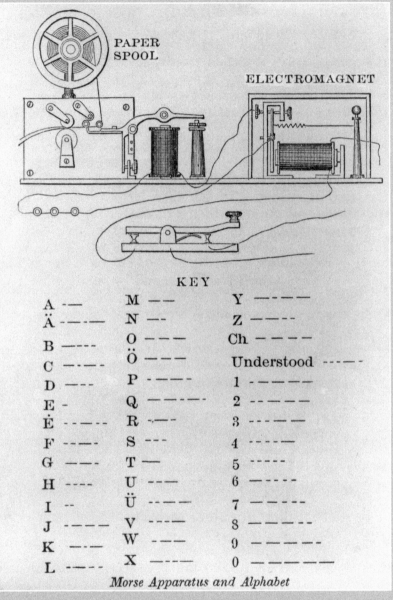

PAPER SPOOL

ELECTROMAGNET

KEY

A	·—	M	——	Y	—·——
Ä	·—·—	N	—·	Z	——··
B	—···	O	———	Ch	————
C	—·—·	Ö	———·	Understood	···—·
D	—··	P	·——·	1	·————
E	·	Q	——·—	2	··———
É	··—··	R	·—·	3	···——
F	··—·	S	···	4	····—
G	——·	T	—	5	·····
H	····	U	··—	6	—····
I	··	Ü	··——	7	——···
J	·———	V	···—	8	———··
K	—·—	W	·——	9	————·
L	·—··	X	—··—	0	—————

Morse Apparatus and Alphabet

Note the telegraph key at the bottom of the diagram. Letters of the received message come through this key and are passed through the electromagnet. Those impulses are then "translated" to marks on the strip of paper from the spool at the left.

determines what is sent and received by each operator. As you can see in the chart, *A* would be sent as *dit-daa* (short-long) and *Z* would be sent as *daa-daa-dit-dit* (long-long-short-short).

It's interesting to note that the most common letters in English have the shortest Morse code equivalents. The letters *E* and *T* are just one character long (*dit* and *daa* respectively), while the letters *A, I, M,* and *N* are each just two characters long. Also, no Morse code letter has more than four characters, and some letters are the reverse of each other. For example, *A* is *dit-daa* and *N* is *daa-dit*.

MacLeod struggled to assemble enough experienced radio operators to transmit convincing messages that would include references to parts of the Fourth Army scattered over Scotland. The radio operators were charged with establishing a pattern and volume of communication that was fitting for such a large, although mostly notional, force. The radio transmissions began on March 22, 1944. By April 6, the whole operation was active.

Messages in World War II were normally sent in a high- or medium-grade cipher. However, because the Allies wanted and expected the Nazi intercept agents to read the Operation SKYE messages, the transmissions had to make sense. In other words, they couldn't just send gibberish as a way to achieve the volume of traffic that would be appropriate for such a large force. The content of the messages needed to fit the operation. For example, if the Nazis intercepted no messages to or from the Royal Army Medical Corps, they would grow suspicious. Beyond that, care needed to be taken that practical questions and information circulated appropriately. Inquiries about matters of pay and allowance should come from the Eighty-Seventh Field Cash Office. The field dressing station would be expected to send and receive messages about medicine and hospital supplies. The wireless operation required "a gigantic volume of fictitious radio signaling."

Here's an example of how a radio transmission program of the Fifty-Second Division worked. From April 7 to April 12, the division maintained radio silence, a usual sign to the intercept squad that something important was imminent. The silence ended with these signals about typical training activities:

April 12: *Assault brigade signal exercise*

April 15: *Assault brigade amphibious exercise*

April 20 and 24: *Two assault brigade amphibious exercises*

May 2–May 4: [radio silence]

May 10: *Divisional amphibious exercise*

These listed exercises were instructions for troops that didn't exist. Of course, the Nazis didn't know that, so intercepts detailing amphibious exercises could only make them more uneasy about a coming invasion.

While the scripts of fictitious messages for each day ran many pages long, they included activities like these of the Fifty-Fifth and Fifty-Eighth Infantry Divisions from June 5, which give an idea of the details required:

0400 hours: *Barrage comes down on Hagshaw Hill.*

0500 hours: *Attack on Hagshaw Hill goes in. 9th South Lancashires supported by the 863rd Field Regiment. Hill held by 6th Highland Light Infantry.*

0700 hours: *Hagshaw Hill captured, but unable advance further. Consolidating. Intend reinforce 9th South Lancashires.*

0900–1100 hours: *Brigade put into counter-attack on Hagshaw Hill, using 5th King's Own Scottish Borderers, supported by 80th Field Regiment 164th Brigade driven off after bitter fighting. Heavy casualties. Brigade not reorganized on line of road running north and south through Douglas.*

These small samples of the bogus radio transmissions that the Nazis overheard offer a glimpse of what was broadcast for a number of months to keep Hitler believing that the notional army was preparing to invade Norway any day.

MacLeod's wireless operation was thorough. Not only did his team send out messages about troop strength and training; it also included convincing messages about the various units that supported the troops. For example, the VII Corps Postal Unit sent messages concerning the delivery of mail to the troops. To prepare for battlefield injuries that would come with the invasion, there were messages from the Fifth Field Dressing Station.

There were also other messages that hinted broadly at where the Fourth Army might be headed. For example, messages were sent to certain officers notifying them that they were to report for ski training. There was a request for suggestions on how to keep gasoline engines running efficiently in cold weather and at high altitudes.

In addition to the wireless messages, MacLeod's deception operatives were skillful at arranging convenient leaks of suggestive information. A Scottish newspaper carried a small story about a soccer match between units in the Fourth Army. A BBC radio reporter told how he spent a day on the training field with a (fictional) division of troops. There was even a lighthearted social note about the recent marriage of a major in the Fourth Army and a member of the women's auxiliary of the VII Corps.

It was not the wireless deception by itself that influenced decisions made by the German high command. The LCS knew that the Nazis were too clever and suspicious to be swayed solely by fake wireless messages and tidbits in the local newspaper—which were, "after all, a familiar British trick." The Germans correctly demanded on-the-scene confirmation of their suspicions about what was going on in Scotland and along the southeast coast of England. Knowing that the Germans would seek additional proof, the British let loose their stable of double agents—assets that had an enormous impact on the success of the FORTITUDE operation. The Abwehr considered these agents most trusted spies. The British, however, knew something about these spies that the Abwehr did not.

The Abwehr *thought* it had spies in place in England. After all, it had sent thirty or forty of them across the channel, and many of them had, in fact, been sending back intelligence reports with regularity. What the Abwehr didn't realize for the duration of the war was that the British had reason to believe that all the spies Germany had sent to England had been quickly captured (or had turned themselves in to MI5) and been turned to work as double agents under the control of a secret deception organization called the Twenty Committee. The committee took its name from the Roman numbers XX: the double cross. Its work marked a dramatic change in the use of double agents.

In the fall of 1940, Hitler sent a handful of spies to England to report to the Abwehr on military and morale matters. It is hard to imagine a group of agents more ill prepared and poorly trained. As James F. Dunnigan and Albert A. Nofi have noted, they were "an eclectic collection of adventurers, misfits, idealists who were willing to compromise." Only a handful were dedicated Nazis, while the others were, like many spies before and since, "variously motivated by greed, adventure, fear, stupidity, and blackmail." The British were able to round them up thanks to intercepted wireless transmissions, and their shortcomings made them suitable pawns to work as double agents. Not every captured spy wound up working for MI5. Some were tried for their crimes and executed, which, no doubt, served notice to the other captured agents that the British expected their cooperation.

The Twenty Committee believed that it was not always the best course of action to capture an enemy agent or eliminate him. The Nazis might then send a more crafty replacement, whom MI5 might not be able to locate. Better, they thought, to keep a troublesome agent under surveillance and impair his usefulness by cutting off his source of important intelligence and by supplying him with what was known as chicken feed—information that was mostly true but only marginally useful, often information that the Germans would eventually find out on their own. The best course was to persuade the spy "by one means or another" to work instead for the opposition. At this last practice, the Twenty Committee was highly skilled, building a roster of double agents whose credibility was, for the most part, unquestioned by the Abwehr for the remainder of the war.

British intelligence believed that it had accounted for all the spies sent by the Nazis because no other spies were mentioned in Nazi communications with the spies in England. Further, the Abwehr seemed content with the fake intelligence that the British were feeding them through the Nazis' own spies.

According to World War II historian Ben Macintyre, up to this point in the war, the double agents had been "used defensively: to catch more spies, obtain information about German military intelligence, and lure the enemy into believing he was running a large and efficient espionage network in Britain." In full swing as part of FORTITUDE NORTH, the work of the double agents of the Twenty Committee marked the "first attempt . . . in the U.K. to organize . . . agents in a balanced and mutually-supporting team" to attain a specific goal and "to plan their part in an operation just as one did that of the forces engaged." The effort was monumental.

A man named Thomas Argyll Robertson coordinated

the secret Twenty Committee. Over time, he realized that "every single German agent in Britain was actually under his control." Such an intelligence triumph allowed the Twenty Committee to use the agents in a more proactive way to feed false and misleading information to their handlers in Hamburg.

Prior to the deception operations of World War II, most deceptions had been the work of individuals rather than an organized effort by a government or military force to deceive the enemy. The same could be said about double agents: their work was temporary and generally connected to a specific battle or operation. Sinon, left behind by the Greeks on the shores of Troy, was responsible for gaining the trust of the Trojans and completing one operation—convincing them to drag the Trojan Horse within the walls of Troy. He succeeded at his bit of treachery and Troy fell. However, the Twenty Committee changed the way double agents worked.

The Twenty Committee—created by B1A, a section of MI5—met for the first time on January 2, 1941. From that point until May 10, 1945, it met every week—that's more than 225 meetings. The band of captured German agents formed the foundation of the Twenty Committee and became another tool to help the Allies maintain FORTITUDE. The D-day Spies, so called because it was believed that their work would help assure the success of the D-day invasion, would deliver to the Axis "all the little lies that together made up the big lie."

As J. C. Masterman, chairman of the Twenty Committee,

later explained, the committee's primary objective was to determine exactly what information could "safely be allowed to pass to the Germans." The secondary objective then became to coordinate the intelligence that was being passed on by the agents. The amount of information delivered by the double agents needed to be catalogued and cross-referenced to prevent one agent from contradicting what another agent said to his handler. At the same time, reports of the double agents could not too closely resemble each other. Although the Abwehr was not a very competent intelligence service, the Allies were justifiably worried that if the Abwehr detected mistakes, the entire deception would unravel. The Germans had shown that they were quick to discredit any information that was contradicted by another credible source, for example, a journalist's report or a reconnaissance plane's images.

The third objective of the Twenty Committee was to compare and coordinate the needs of different intelligence departments and resolve any conflicts among them. The Twenty Committee directed a large and complicated operation that included representatives from MI5, MI6, the navy, the air force, the Home Office (army), and the Foreign Office (national security), among others. It was not unheard of that various departments and personalities would clash in times of national crisis.

Although the British were quite successful at finding Nazi agents, developing a double agent takes time and resources. As Masterman wrote after the war, "A double agent cannot be summoned from the vasty [sic] deep and set upon the stage ready at once to play a leading role. He must be steadily and cautiously 'built up' in reputation and that is a process which lasted always for months and often for years." During this time of learning and training, the double-agent-to-be was often more a liability than an asset to the committee. While the double agents were the foundation of the FORTITUDE deception, they were, in a sense, only the proverbial tip of the iceberg. The support system necessary for an agent's success needed to be extensive and committed to the deception. It was the support staff that created the misinformation that would be transmitted and decided who would transmit which information.

Once a double agent was recruited and trained by the Twenty Committee, a support system was put into place around that agent. He would receive a complete life story, a story that would keep neighbors and acquaintances from getting too curious. MI5 created documents to support the life story, such as an identity card, a wartime ration card for food and supplies, and a clothing coupon. The agent also received a place to live.

With a cover story established, the agent was assigned a full-time case officer to "control and organize" the agent and his wireless transmissions. In addition to the case officer, a wireless operator monitored the messages an agent sent. If the agent could not be trusted to send and receive his own messages, the wireless operator would actually send the messages on his behalf. If the double agent sent transmissions himself, the British wireless operator on the team studied his methods, including his style and mannerisms, because a wireless operator's touch on the Morse code key is just as unique as his handwriting or his voice. In the event that a British operator needed to take over for the double agent, the operator had to be able to mimic the style and quirks of the double agent, lest the German handlers notice the change in the agent's "fist."

"Fist" is the term for the manner in which an operator sends a message with his key. The telegraph operators sending messages for the double agents of the Twenty Committee needed to be careful of their fist. It's difficult for two operators to send "perfect code," since each would be ever so slightly different from another operator sending the exact same word, character, or number.

When a telegraph operator "talks" to the same person on a radio over and over for months or even years, the other person can learn his sending pattern and know that what he is receiving is coming from the same person. Still, this was never a significant worry among the Twenty telegraph operators. For one thing, they were all similarly trained and would guard against the chance of their fist betraying them. Another reason the Twenty operators were not worried about differences in the fist of various operators is that the Germans clearly believed that they were receiving legitimate intelligence from their spies in England. There were no Bletchley intercepts that suggested that the Germans were suspicious of the manner in which the messages were transmitted.

The British operators were trained by experts who followed basic guidelines for becoming proficient in Morse code. Beyond stressing the importance of practice, they understood that to learn Morse, a person needed to hear it. However, a problem often developed when trainees used paper and pencil to write each letter as it was sent, as opposed to learning to copy complete words. Experts recommended that operators learn to hear the unique rhythm and sound of a word, much the way one learns words as a child. By listening to the words, the operators learned to go beyond individual letters and listen for complete thoughts. They were encouraged to learn Morse code the same way they would learn a foreign language—by listening. The general rule drummed into new operators was: "Break the pencil and toss out the paper."

In addition to a case officer and wireless operator, a double agent's team usually included two guards, each working a twelve-hour shift; an officer with a car; a housekeeper; and someone who would cook for the agent and other members of the agent's team. A good case officer's life was intense. He had to "live the case with the agent . . . see with the agent's eyes and hear with the ears of his agent," according to J. C. Masterman, chairman of the committee.

The double agent had to be alert to the kinds of things

the handlers asked of their spies. Such queries might shed light on what moves the Germans were considering or, in fact, planning. For example, if a double agent was asked to find out about the defenses of an airfield on the south coast of England, they could assume that the Luftwaffe was considering an attack on the airfield. Knowing this possibility, the British could deceive the Nazis with false intelligence. They could send information that the airfield was well protected, perhaps causing the Luftwaffe to rethink its attack. Or the agent could offer fake information that the airfield was only minimally protected, which could be an invitation for the Luftwaffe to be caught in an RAF ambush when they attacked.

Keeping a very careful and exact record of each case was of the utmost importance. All the traffic between a double agent and his case officer was documented. The same needed to be done for conversations, as well as trips the agent made and actions he took. Such careful records—and this was well before electronic databases—were important so that any notional stories the agent might use would include convincing details that appeared to be true.

The work of spies is often compartmentalized to protect the overall operation. A Twenty Committee agent would know his case officer, of course, but would have no contact with other spies who were part of FORTITUDE. So while a double agent could potentially betray his British handler, he would not be able to implicate any of the other Twenty Committee agents.

Deceptive intelligence is generally more effective when it is fed to the enemy in small doses from a number of different sources, giving the enemy the chance to fit the pieces of the puzzle together and see the picture. "The great lie," historian Ben Macintyre has noted, "would be made up of snippets, gleanings, and hints, a mosaic."

While the Twenty Committee happily accepted Germans who were willing to spy, it did not waste time attempting the reverse. In other words, the committee was against the idea of taking a British agent and trying to get the Germans to accept him as a double agent. Such attempts were only rarely successful. The Twenty Committee was content to turn the agents that Germany sent to England. It is hard to argue with the success that it had doing just that.

As far as MI5 was concerned, it was imperative that the double agent live the life his country thought he was living. Even though the double agent was living a lie and sending intelligence that was misleading or false, the Twenty Committee believed that it was necessary for a double agent to visit the sites he was describing to his handler. It was, in the eyes of the committee, "an imperative necessity" that the agent "actually experience all that he professes to have done." Whenever possible, the agent was to tell the truth and follow the instructions of his German handlers.

If an agent proved ineffective or troublesome, he would be removed from the deception operation. Records indicate that a number of the agents were, in fact, withdrawn from service. For example, an agent code-named Careless was no longer used after eighteen months of service when he "refused to continue to work." Giraffe was removed because of "insufficient traffic." With other agents ready to be part of the deception, such changes rarely posed a problem for the Twenty Committee. The outgoing agent's wireless operator would transmit a short message—something like, "They are on to me"—and disappear. Spies on both sides dropped out of action all the time. And since the Germans paid their agents in England via couriers, MI5 would occasionally arrest a courier who was to meet an agent to make a payment. The agent could then send an indignant message—"I haven't been paid. No more."—and no longer transmit.

According to J. C. Masterman's records, the Twenty Committee agents who served for the longest amount of time were:

Brutus	October 1941–January 1945
Garbo	April 1942–May 1945
Tate	September 1940–May 1945
Tricycle	December 1940–May 1944
Mutt	April 1941–May 1944
Jeff	April 1941–May 1944

With their stable of double agents, a crucial task of the special means staff was to decide which of the Twenty agents should report on which part of the mostly notional army in Scotland and other areas. Brutus and Garbo were the "first violins" of the operation, the agents most relied on by the Committee. Brutus was given the main responsibility for reporting on the Scottish order of battle and the locations of the troops. An agent named Freak would report from Northern Ireland, where, according to his cover story, he worked as a military attaché. As such, he would have access to the details of the order of battle in that part of the U.K. And finally, Garbo—the Twenty Committee's most prolific agent—would report on naval exercises near Glasgow, where he told Hamburg he lived. Of course, these agents were usually nowhere near where they claimed they were. All, in fact, worked in London, in a room at Norfolk House in an affluent section of the city.

The double agents, at the instructions of their case officers, provided the Germans with what their handlers believed to be accurate and invaluable intelligence about the Allied order of battle. But because the information was fictitious, it was worthless to the Germans. Worse, it caused them to make critically wrong decisions. For the Allies, on the other hand, the "controlled leakage," as it was called, was invaluable to them because the Germans reacted to it in a way that weakened their defenses at Normandy.

Every intelligence agency strives to get the order of battle of enemy forces. This order of battle includes the number of troops and other personnel in a certain army. It also tells where the forces are located.

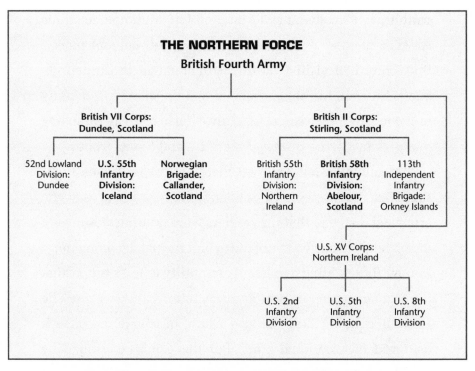

THE NORTHERN FORCE

British Fourth Army

British VII Corps:
Dundee, Scotland

52nd Lowland
Division:
Dundee

**U.S. 55th
Infantry
Division:
Iceland**

**Norwegian
Brigade:
Callander,
Scotland**

British II Corps:
Stirling, Scotland

British 55th
Infantry
Division:
Northern
Ireland

**British 58th
Infantry
Division:
Abelour,
Scotland**

113th
Independent
Infantry
Brigade:
Orkney Islands

U.S. XV Corps:
Northern Ireland

U.S. 2nd
Infantry
Division

U.S. 5th
Infantry
Division

U.S. 8th
Infantry
Division

*This chart contains information that was intentionally leaked to the Germans by
Allied double agents. Here, the formations that were notional, or fictitious, are
set in boldface type. That distinction was not made in the leaked document.*

Roger Hesketh wrote shortly after the war that before
FORTITUDE NORTH began, the Germans believed three
things about the Allies: that the fictional British Fourth Army
existed; that the Fifty-Second Lowland Division was in eastern Scotland; and (thanks to the reports of double agents
Cobweb and Beetle) that the U.S. Fifty-Fifth Division was in
Iceland, within striking distance of Norway. Hesketh concluded, "We owed our flying start directly to [these] preoccu-
pations, but partly also to the uncontrolled [double] agents."

The Twenty Committee used a pair of "second violin"

double agents code-named Mutt and Jeff. Mutt contacted his Abwehr handler with news that a Russian colonel named Budyonny had visited the British command in Edinburgh, Scotland. Mutt further speculated that the visit of Budyonny indicated that some sort of joint invasion of Norway was being planned, involving British, American, and Soviet troops.

Meanwhile, Jeff reported that "hundreds, maybe thousands" of troops were in Scotland. He also noted that the arm patch insignia that the soldiers were wearing was new to him. The Germans were unable to find the patch among those in their files, adding a touch of credibility to Jeff's report that the army amassing in Scotland was indeed a new army. The Abwehr couldn't find the arm patch, of course, because it belonged to a notional army. But the patch mentioned by Jeff shows how the LCS and the U.S. Army went to great lengths to make sure the small details of FORTITUDE were not overlooked.

In fact, to make sure that information on the arm patch found its way to the public, and eventually to the Nazis, the army arranged for *National Geographic* to do a feature article on U.S. Army insignias. The article, of course, included photographs of a number of insignias and arm patches. The army made sure that several of the notional arm patches were among those photographed. A handful of magazines were printed before the army stopped the presses. At that point, the article was edited to exclude the notional arm patches.

As luck would have it, one of the unedited copies of

the magazine found its way to the desk of "an enterprising capitalist down on Seventh Avenue (New York City's 'Fashion Avenue,')" according to Albert A. Nofi. This entrepreneur produced samples of the patches in the hope of landing a fat government contract. The army quickly bought thousands of them and issued them to soldiers who were shipping out to Europe from New York City. In "one way or another the Germans soon got wind of the 'existence' of these formations."

The Twenty Committee then turned to Garbo to contact his handlers. He reported to them that he'd sent one of his best operatives, Benedict—there was no such person—to investigate. Benedict had reported that the insignia of the troops he noticed—"a shell on a dark background"—was "completely unknown" to him. He added that he saw troops exercising in arctic clothing.

Garbo offered his opinion to Hamburg—it was really his case officer providing the opinion—that he was convinced that the Allies were, in fact, planning two major offensives for about the same time, early June 1944. He felt certain that the Allies would cross the North Sea and invade Norway. Garbo also told his handlers in Hamburg that the Allies were massing troops in the East Anglia region of England for an invasion of France at Pas-de-Calais, a key ingredient of FORTITUDE SOUTH.

A minor part of FORTITUDE NORTH was physical deception, a tactic that the British had used to their advantage in the battle of El Alamein. Since Germany had lost the 1940

Battle of Britain for air supremacy over the British Isles, the Royal Air Force had kept the Luftwaffe at a distance from England. Although the Germans still ran routine reconnaissance flights at thirty thousand feet over the Orkney and Shetland Islands off the northern coast of Scotland, the planners of FORTITUDE NORTH believed there was no real need for physical deception on the scale of the elaborate dummy tanks and decoy buildings used in the battle of El Alamein.

A dummy plane similar to the ones used in Scotland

However, "hundreds of twin-engine aircraft . . . began to appear on Scottish airfields," including Peterhead and Fraserburgh, on Scotland's northeast coast. These dummy planes were the remnants of Operation TINDALL, an unsuccessful 1943 deception scheme for an invasion of Norway. Using wood, canvas, and metal tubing, England's remarkable *camoufleurs* had constructed dozens of fake fighter planes and twin-engine bombers. This "air force" was built at night to minimize the chances that the fake planes would be discovered in the act of being built.

Because German reconnaissance flights were permitted occasionally to stray over these sites, they were dressed up for added authenticity. Dummy fuel trucks and other vehicles were parked near the runways, and other airfield dummy equipment and supplies created the impression of activity, giving the Nazis more evidence that the Allies were serious about the invasion of Norway. This bit of physical deception in FORTITUDE NORTH "may have contributed a little to the overall success of the deception," but was not nearly as pivotal as the special means ops.

In reality, the British did not have anything *near* the forces needed to invade Norway and do battle with the overwhelming strength that the Nazis had at the ready in the country. But that did not stop the British from sending small commando bands to Norway to carry out audacious raids against Nazi army bases and industrial sites. The purpose of these attacks within the context of FORTITUDE NORTH was to have the Wehrmacht view them as pre-invasion raids, a sign of what was to come. And the British could not overlook the fact that the raids actually did significant damage to the sources of Nazi supplies in Norway.

On the diplomatic front, the British created something of a black propaganda op with Operation Graffham, another part of FORTITUDE NORTH, aimed at Norway's neutral neighbor, Sweden. Graffham was designed to put pressure on

Sweden. The British wanted access to Sweden's airspace, as well as to its airfields and ports. They also wanted to let the Swedish government know that if it wanted to reap some of the benefits of the coming defeat of the Third Reich, it needed to cut all ties with Germany. The Allies were especially interested in ending the sale of ball bearings by the Swedes to Germany, since these were an essential component of so many war machines, including airplanes, tanks, and armored troop carriers.

The English ambassador journeyed to Sweden and held a meeting with the embassy staff, knowing that his comments would find their way to the Germans. He said that the British had "always had good relations with our Swedish friends and hope that these will remain so. We must, however, reckon with the possibility that this good relationship will be put to the test. We can no longer calmly look on while neutral countries deliver goods to our enemies, which do us harm." The ambassador went on to say that deliveries of iron ore and ball bearings "must not continue in the future. We must find suitable ways to prevent it." While the threat to the Swedish government was clear, the British were also putting the Germans on notice that their supply of crucial material from Sweden was likely to end.

FORTITUDE NORTH didn't officially conclude until September 30, 1944—several months after D-day. It ended when the Combined Chiefs of Staff believed that the Germans could no longer afford to keep so many troops in areas not actively engaged in the war effort, like Scandinavia. And with the diminished Nazi presence in Norway, the Allies felt that the "cost of maintaining such threats would no longer justify the effort required." By the end of June, real and notional divisions of the Fourth Army that hadn't been moved for D-day itself were transferred, some to become main cogs in FORTITUDE SOUTH.

When FORTITUDE NORTH was shut down, General "Bulgy" Thorne, the commander of the invisible Fourth Army, said, "As time went on we found it hard to separate the real from the imaginary. The feeling that the Fourth Army really existed and the fact that it was holding the German troops immobilized made one almost believe in its reality." The Nazi high command certainly believed that the Fourth Army was real, and the Allies used many of the same deception techniques in a parallel operation, FORTITUDE SOUTH, the deception plan that covered Operation NEPTUNE, the amphibious invasion of Normandy.

By the early months of 1944, the Germans were worried about an invasion of Norway. The successful deception caused the Wehrmacht to keep a quarter of a million troops in the country when far fewer were needed to control the territory. That meant that two hundred fifty thousand troops were not available to reinforce their brothers-in-arms when the Allied troops hit the beaches at Normandy.

CHAPTER 6

FORTITUDE SOUTH

Although FORTITUDE NORTH and FORTITUDE SOUTH were two separate operations with deceptions in different parts of the United Kingdom, it's important to remember that they were simultaneous operations with the same goal: fooling Hitler and the German high command about the place and date of Operation NEPTUNE, the huge amphibious assault at Normandy. While the invasion was set for early June, FORTITUDE SOUTH, the "crown jewel of the BODYGUARD deception," was meant to convince Hitler that the real invasion target was Pas-de-Calais, and that the attack would come nearly seven weeks after the real invasion.

All aspects of FORTITUDE SOUTH, including its six QUICKSILVER operations, needed to point in the same direction. If they worked as planned, Hitler would keep two of his best armies in Pas-de-Calais even once Normandy was attacked. And, as history shows, FORTITUDE SOUTH did exactly what it was supposed to do. The Nazis bought the lie, opening western Europe to the invasion that would end Hitler's plan for the conquest of Europe.

Without a doubt, FORTITUDE SOUTH was far more complicated than FORTITUDE NORTH, involving more operations and hundreds of thousands of people, from the men and women at Bletchley Park who broke enciphered German wireless transmissions to the soldiers who stormed the beach at Normandy and parachuted into France. Charles Cruickshank called it the "largest, most elaborate, most carefully planned, most vital and most successful of all the Allied deceptive operations," utilizing the "years of experience gained in every branch of deceptive arts." FORTITUDE SOUTH used many of the same techniques applied in FORTITUDE NORTH and earlier operations. Many of the methods had been around since ancient times, including visual deception, as well as the use of double agents and a notional army. However, the geography of this operation called for a more extensive use of visual deception and the creation of a much larger notional army.

To get the Nazis to believe that the invasion of Europe, which both sides knew was inevitable, would take place at Pas-de-Calais, the Allies needed to create an army that would be large enough to be seen as a credible threat, without actually removing any of the Allied soldiers from Operation

NEPTUNE. Earlier in the war, Operation COCKADE, another deception about an Allied invasion of Europe, had failed because the Germans knew that the Allies didn't have the manpower in England to carry out such an invasion. FORTITUDE SOUTH needed to convincingly create that illusion.

Fabricating the force that the Nazis would be anticipating at Pas-de-Calais became the centerpiece of FORTITUDE SOUTH. If the invasion force was not believable, the whole deception would unravel. The stakes were high. If the invasion failed, so would any hope of defeating Hitler.

One of the things that the Allies had in their favor in planning FORTITUDE SOUTH was that Pas-de-Calais truly was a good choice for an invasion. First of all, it was a mere twenty miles from Dover, England, the shortest crossing point between England and France. The short distance was advantageous to the Allies. It would allow RAF fighter planes to protect a landing force all the way from England to France. It would also give the landing crafts the opportunity to make several trips each day with troops and supplies. Finally, an invading force landing at the beaches of Pas-de-Calais would have a shorter route to Berlin than an army landing down the coast at Normandy.

An invasion at Pas-de-Calais made sense in two additional ways: It furnished a deep-water port, which the Allies would welcome for the vessels that were providing logistic support to the troops. In addition, the Nazi buzz-bomb (forerunner of a cruise missile) launch sites were located near

Pas-de-Calais, giving them a shorter flight to London than from Germany. An invading Allied army would certainly target these launch sites as part of its mission. FORTITUDE SOUTH needed only to build on the Nazis' predisposition to worry about Pas-de-Calais as the logical invasion point.

The cover and deception plan created to protect the secrets of the First United States Army Group (FUSAG), a mostly notional force, and the bogus invasion at Pas-de-Calais was code-named QUICKSILVER and featured six operations. Although some of the QUICKSILVER operations were more complicated than others, each was part of a package deal to fool Hitler and the Nazi high command. The parts of QUICKSILVER were:

- **QUICKSILVER I:** The story that the Allied force, the notional FUSAG, would invade at Pas-de-Calais
- **QUICKSILVER II:** A wireless radio deception that would provide the Nazis with the information that Allies wanted them to know
- **QUICKSILVER III:** The show of landing craft— some real but mostly fake—along the east and southeast coast of England
- **QUICKSILVER IV:** The aerial bombardment of Pas-de-Calais and nearby communication facilities as an indication that the area was being "softened up" for the coming invasion
- **QUICKSILVER V:** The creation of a buzz of activity

in the Dover area, including new radio networks, all meant to call attention to Dover as an embarkation point for the troops who would invade Pas-de-Calais

- **QUICKSILVER VI:** The creation of "fake lighting schemes" along the south coast of England to fool the Nazis

By far the most complicated part of the huge Fortitude deception was QUICKSILVER I, establishing an army that the Germans would believe to be a realistic threat to cross the channel and invade France at Pas-de-Calais. Like its counterpart in Scotland, FORTITUDE SOUTH began its fiction of FUSAG by selecting a commander of the notional forces. Once again, the Allies were looking for a military leader who was held in high regard by the Nazis, a commander who would be placed in charge of such a very important operation. In the eyes of Dwight D. Eisenhower, supreme commander of Allied forces in Europe, there was only one person for the job: General George S. Patton ("Old Blood and Guts," as he was known), fresh from his triumphs in North Africa and Sicily. However, there was another reason that Eisenhower decided to have Patton command FUSAG: Patton was in trouble.

In 1943, when Patton was visiting a field hospital in Sicily, talking to wounded soldiers, he came upon a young infantryman who was slouched on a stool, suffering from what was then called battle fatigue and is now known as

"Old Blood and Guts": General George S. Patton

post-traumatic stress disorder. When the general asked the soldier where he was injured, the soldier replied that he wasn't wounded. He just couldn't take any more fighting. Patton whipped out his gloves and slapped the soldier in the face with them. He then ordered the soldier out of the hospital tent and back to his unit.

A "media firestorm" followed, with politicians and journalists demanding Patton's court-martial. President Roosevelt labeled his conduct "reprehensible." Eisenhower himself thought that Patton's actions were "despicable." At the same time, Eisenhower well understood Patton's value as an effective and aggressive commander. Eisenhower proposed a compromise. He would not court-martial Patton if he served as the commander of a notional army group that would be part of FORTITUDE. Patton fumed at being shuffled off to the sidelines to command an army group that didn't even exist. However, Eisenhower made it clear that if Patton served well in his FUSAG role, the supreme commander would see to it that he returned to command the Third U.S. Army in France following the D-day invasion. Patton realized that if he wanted to lead a real army again, he had no choice but to accept Eisenhower's deal.

Eisenhower knew full well that the Nazis, after battling Patton in North Africa and Sicily, held him in high esteem. The Nazis would take notice that Patton was in command of an army group. With Old Blood and Guts at the helm, the FUSAG would be the army to invade France. By keeping tabs on where Patton was, the Nazis would have a good idea of where the Allies would land in France. And, with Patton leading the FUSAG, all signs pointed to Pas-de-Calais.

With a commanding officer selected, the FUSAG was activated on October 10, 1943. By May it included the Third U.S. Army, with nine divisions (about one hundred thirty-five thousand men), and the First Canadian, with two divisions (about thirty thousand men). The army was located in southeast England, around Dover, adding credibility to the idea that this army group was preparing for a cross-channel invasion of Pas-de-Calais. While there were real troops in the early days of the FUSAG, that gradually changed as men were moved to the Portsmouth area in southern England, the embarkation point for the Normandy invasion. The troops that departed were gradually replaced by notional troops. By the end of August 1943, "virtually the whole original FUSAG was fictitious."

One of the details that was given careful scrutiny in the creation of the notional army was the selection of men who should command under Patton. Names could not simply be invented, because the German Wehrmacht kept detailed files on Allied commanders, including their military histories as well as their battlefield tendencies, especially their strengths and weaknesses. When the list of Allied commanders under Patton was compiled, it was leaked to the Germans through secret channels.

QUICKSILVER I was an "elaborate masquerade on a colossal scale." The other QUICKSILVER deceptions were created to support the "big lie" of the FUSAG. And since the Nazis had essentially three means of gaining intelligence about the invasion—aerial reconnaissance, spies, and signal intercepts—the QUICKSILVER deceptions were designed to thwart such intelligence gathering.

In support of the QUICKSILVER deceptions, the Allies also had two significant factors on their side. These were the crucial work of special means (the double agents of the Twenty Committee) and the feedback from radio intercepts deciphered by the code breakers at Bletchley Park, who had worked long and hard to crack the messages sent by the Germans' Enigma machine, a system the Nazis considered unbreakable. This intelligence—with the code name of ULTRA—served the Allies well in the entire operation.

Each of Patton's notional divisions had a similar makeup of a few hundred men. Two dozen signal corps personnel were assigned to create a division's worth of radio traffic. The other members of each division were mostly engineers, charged with the work required to keep up the charade of the fake army. These engineers maintained and operated dummy camps. For example, they took care of numerous inflatable tanks and trucks that served as decoys for any aerial reconnaissance, making sure that they kept their shapes and remained anchored to the ground until it was time to move them. There were buildings and tents that needed to be kept from falling into disrepair. The engineers also cared for the audio equipment that broadcast the sounds that would be heard in camps of such size: truck engines, generators, and even the sounds of men and equipment preparing for the invasion at Pas-de-Calais.

BLETCHLEY PARK

THE CODE-BREAKING operation at Bletchley Park began in the spring of 1938, when the Bletchley estate—consisting of elaborate mansions and fifty-five acres of grounds about fifty miles from London—was bought by someone who claimed that it was to be "converted into an air defense training school." In August of 1939, "groups of rather odd, mainly middle-aged men" and a number of young women began arriving. That was only the beginning. By the end of the war, twelve thousand workers passed through Bletchley Park, nine thousand at the height of the code-breaking efforts in January 1945. Connected by rail lines to some of the U.K.'s premier universities—Oxford, Cambridge, and Aberdeen—Bletchley's location allowed MI6 to cast its recruiting net to attract some of the brightest minds for its operations.

Bletchley Park did not buzz with the activities of spies and intelligence agents. Rather, the men and women—80 percent of the workers at Bletchley Park were female—spoke many languages, excelled at mathematics and chess, and were crossword-puzzle wizards. Most of what the code breakers did was not strictly a matter of mathematics or science. In the words of one technology historian, it required someone with "an overalertness to relatively unimportant or tangential aspects of problems."

Bletchley Park, site of Allied code-breaking operations

In 1941, the Government Codes and Cypher School advertised a competition to find those who could solve the fiendishly
clever crossword puzzle in the *Daily Telegraph* in less than twelve
minutes. People flocked to the contest, unaware that they were
auditioning for a position at Bletchley. After the contest, MI6
made discreet inquiries of those with the best puzzle-solving
times and, in many cases, recruited those men and women to
be part of the code-breaking team at the estate in the British
countryside.

The mission of the team at Bletchley Park was to crack Nazi codes and ciphers, many of which were transmitted using the Germans' famed Enigma machines. These portable cipher machines with rotor scramblers were immensely difficult to crack. However, the Nazis didn't know that the Polish cipher bureau had cracked Enigma in 1932 while the German army was still testing the machine. The Poles later built a working replica of an Enigma machine and gave it to MI6 before the Nazis invaded Poland. The Nazis did change components of the original cipher machine, but Poland's work went a long way toward Bletchley's development of Colossus, the "world's first semi-programmable electronic computer."

It was apparent from the start that the Bletchley Park mansion would never be large enough to accommodate the thousands of men and women needed for this valuable work. Consequently, more than thirty wooden huts and several concrete blocks lined the estate grounds. The huts were numbered, while a letter identified each block. For example, the workers in Hut 4 worked on naval intelligence, specifically analysis of naval Enigma intercepts. Italian air and naval intercepts and Japanese intercepts were tackled in Block B.

One of the most remarkable things about Bletchley Park, or Station X, as it was code-named, is the extraordinary security that existed, not only during the war when security was one of the keys to a successful intelligence operation, but for thirty years *after* the war. In fact, Bletchley Park was virtually unknown to the public until 1974 when F. W. Winterbotham broke the silence in his book *The Ultra Secret.* That book opened the flood-gates for other books on the code-breaking operation, although many Station X workers took their secrets to the grave, still feeling bound by the Official Secrets Act they signed, swearing themselves to silence about what went on at Station X.

In addition to the invaluable role Bletchley Park played in the success of Operation OVERLORD, the code breakers played a significant role in Allied battlefield successes in North Africa. Their efforts also helped to put an end to the destruction and loss of life inflicted on all manner of shipping by the submarines of the German navy.

Because the Allies were fearful that the Germans would realize that Axis losses in battle were the result of the break-ing of Enigma, they created a notional network of spies code-named "Boniface." Allied intelligence agents left enough tanta-lizing clues to point to "Boniface" as a spy ring at work within Germany.

It's difficult to quantify how the successes of Station X code breakers influenced the war. However, Sir Harry Hinsley, who worked at Bletchley Park from 1939 until the end of the war and became the official historian of British intelligence in the war, said, "My own conclusion is that it shortened the war by not less than two years and probably by four years—that is, the war in the Atlantic, the Mediterranean and Europe."

In addition to the engineers, the camps included a number of set designers and artists with similar skills who had been recruited from theatrical and movie studios to assist the engineers. These men designed and built fake aircraft, tanks, and other equipment that wasn't inflatable.

While the FUSAG was taking shape, the real invasion army was also gaining strength. Concealing an army of more than a million troops and support personnel from an enemy that was but a short distance away on the other side of the English Channel demanded absolute security. This is easier said than done in most instances, but, in this case, the Allies managed to maintain tight security for months leading up to the D-day invasion and beyond.

By the time FORTITUDE was put into operation, England's Royal Air Force controlled the skies around the British Isles, so the only Luftwaffe reconnaissance planes that got close enough to snoop were those that the RAF allowed to fly over because the Twenty Committee wanted the Nazis to have visual confirmation of some aspect of QUICKSILVER.

While MI5 worked very hard to capture German spies as they landed in England, it also needed to guard against the innocent verbal slip of citizens who lived in or visited the east and southeast sections of England, where the fake army was stationed, as well as the southwest section of the country, where the real invasion army was gathering for embarkation. With such a large area of the country occupied with military operations, the Allies were understandably worried that a careless remark about what someone saw could find its way to Germany and threaten the whole operation.

In an effort to control security, the British established an exclusion zone ten miles deep that ran from Land's End, at the most southwesterly tip of England, all the way to the Wash, a shallow bay on the North Sea side of England.

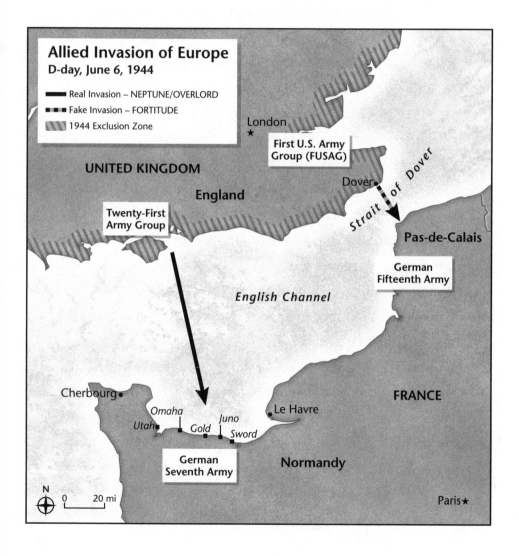

Allied Invasion of Europe
D-day, June 6, 1944

- Real Invasion – NEPTUNE/OVERLORD
- Fake Invasion – FORTITUDE
- 1944 Exclusion Zone

London
First U.S. Army Group (FUSAG)

UNITED KINGDOM

England

Twenty-First Army Group

Dover

Strait of Dover

Pas-de-Calais

German Fifteenth Army

English Channel

Cherbourg

Omaha
Utah
Gold
Juno
Sword

Le Havre

FRANCE

German Seventh Army

Normandy

N
0   20 mi

Paris ★

This security zone was designed to exclude all visitors. However, the ban allowed so many exceptions that it became less than airtight. On one hand, visits had to be made by train, which could be easily policed. But visits were permitted for "business purposes, weddings and funerals, [and] to see people over 70 who were dangerously ill." With such exceptions, it's easy to see how an enemy agent could have infiltrated the area to gather intelligence. Although they didn't know it, the Nazis had no genuine agents on hand.

The security was made tighter by the "unprecedented step" of imposing censorship on foreign diplomats in London, which included diplomatic communications inside England. Such measures caused an uproar in London. They were considered "distinctly un-British and were called into question by everyone, Churchill included." The problem was that the Allied command could not explain that such measures were not merely a precaution because of the war, but were deemed essential to preserve the secrecy of FORTITUDE.

The coast of England was roughly divided into two sections, with Portsmouth being the dividing point. Each section had its own strategic demands that needed to be met. All in all, the situation facing the LCS was tricky. They had a fake army in the east and southeast that they wanted the Germans to know about. But in the south and southwest they had a real invasion force that they needed desperately to keep secret.

The section to the west was a "maximum concealment

area." Camouflage work in progress was halted, for fear that if the Germans saw progress in an area that they had already observed from the air, they would become suspicious and perhaps try to get a closer look. New camouflage was permitted, but, as Cruickshank has noted, "would be hidden as far as was humanly possible." All campsites and assembly points needed to be concealed, with every step taken to hide the presence of troops. "Tents must be darkened, smokeless stoves used in the cookhouses, khaki towels issued instead of white."

In the east, on the other hand, the problem was the opposite. The Allies needed to make the "presence" of the fake FUSAG seem realistic and credible without overplaying their hand. It was a monstrous undertaking, involving artists, engineers, scientists, and carpenters. Large tent cities sprung up in the countryside. Cookstoves were kept burning, even though nothing was cooking. Dirt roads were cut among the tents, some leading into the woods, but "from the air these same roads looked to lead to concealed ammo dumps, headquarters or staging areas."

Unlike FORTITUDE NORTH, this operation made extensive use of inflatable vehicles. Entire battalions of "blow-up tanks, guns, and trucks in assembly-like areas appeared quite real" to Luftwaffe pilots miles above the countryside. A local legend tells of a farmer's bull riled by an inflatable Sherman tank in his field. The story claims that the bull charged the tank as the horrified farmer looked on, expecting the worst when his bull hit the vehicle. To his surprise, this tank lost out to the bull and was rushed for an emergency repair!

An inflatable dummy tank used in FORTITUDE SOUTH

Along with the tents for the soldiers, encampments included other facilities: dining hall, hospital, ammunition depot, and "even sewage treatment farms." And, of course, an army of that size needed fuel depots and parking lots lined with tanks, jeeps, and ambulances. Most of the vehicles were merely dummies made of fabric and wood. Yet they couldn't remain static. That would surely look suspicious to any observation planes. So the camouflage team moved a portion of the fake vehicles, always under cover of darkness, so no one would see them carrying fake tanks and trucks from one part of the field to another.

There was, however, one detail lacking in this scene of inflatable dummies created by the *camoufleurs*. Inflatable tanks and trucks did not, of course, make any tracks when they were moved, an oversight that could have doomed the deception had it been picked up by a perceptive observer. The deceivers invented a solution. They dragged specially designed tire-and-tread devices that left plenty of marks on the roads and in the fields that would look, to the Luftwaffe, like the marks left by heavy tank and truck traffic.

QUICKSILVER II, the radio deception component of FORTITUDE SOUTH, mirrored a similar operation that was part of FORTITUDE NORTH. With southern coastal England so close to the listening posts that the Nazi Y Service had established, the Germans had no trouble intercepting the fake transmissions and deciphering messages that were intentionally written in an easy-to-break code. As with other aspects of FORTITUDE, the Allies had the benefit of the Ultra intelligence to confirm that the Nazis had, in fact, intercepted and broken the wireless transmissions.

Since the main purpose of QUICKSILVER was to allow the Germans to gain intelligence about the makeup and operation of the FUSAG, a "blizzard of simulated radio traffic" flew back and forth among the divisions in Patton's mostly notional army. At the high point of the deception, there were twenty-two formations supporting the existence of the FUSAG. Each of the radio operators was issued an "eight-inch-thick book of scripted radio transmissions." The wireless operators used the scripts to create realistic chatter for the snooping Y Service agents. As the wireless teams did in FORTITUDE NORTH, FUSAG radiomen drove around the countryside transmitting their messages. The Number 5 Wireless Group was equipped to "mimic the traffic of a corps of three divisions, from vans each of which could simulate the traffic of six transmitters representing a division and its component brigade. Its voice traffic was prerecorded on wire recorders."

Military police continually broadcast reports of disorderly soldiers in the southern towns. The MPs also broadcast news of the movement of large convoys of trucks and equipment. By the time QUICKSILVER II was shut down, "13,358 phony messages would have been sent by the Americans alone, averaging 230 a day."

Another example of the eye for details that the Allied deceivers used skillfully was the submission of letters to the editors of local newspapers in southeast England. Writers complained that the "massive influx of foreign troops was having an enormous negative impact on the citizenry." An LCS agent wrote a letter in the guise of a local minister about the decline of morals "among young British women since the arrival of the American and Canadian troops."

The complaints didn't stop with fake letters about the behavior of make-believe troops. Other "townspeople" across the area railed about how the convoys of military vehicles kicked up so much dust that laundry on clotheslines had to be washed again. And, of course, there were the inevitable complaints about the reckless and rude American soldiers behind the wheels of these vehicles. Double agents made sure that copies of such letters found their way to Lisbon, where they were rerouted to the Abwehr headquarters in Berlin. These offered more proof, the agents claimed, for the buildup of American and Canadian troops in the area near Dover.

Tent cities sprang up far and wide in East Anglia. As one historian has noted, "Fakery had become an immense industry in the interests of FORTITUDE and QUICKSILVER." East Anglia took on the look and feel of "an enormous film lot." However, the presence of FUSAG troops would not be enough to fool the Nazis. Some members of the Twenty-First Army Group were dissatisfied with the deception efforts. These officers felt that, while the tent cities with their inflatable tanks and trucks were all well and good, the Nazi high command would base its "conclusions about the direction and scale of the coming assault not on the camps and kindred evidence, but simply on the shipping in the ports." This concern was addressed by QUICKSILVER III.

QUICKSILVER III was designed to create a hectic and crowded scene on the rivers and harbors of East Anglia. Four hundred "landing ships, each in reality little more than tubular scaffolding, canvas and wood floating on oil drums," had been built at a film studio near London and trucked to launch sites.

These fake landing ships needed to look authentic from the air, so steps were taken to fool the Luftwaffe: "Galley fires were simulated by burning tow, oil was spread around, clothes lines were put up and washing hung out." The

Fake supply barges in East Anglia

camoufleurs completed the picture with sufficient lights burning at night to indicate the presence of men hard at work, loading the ships and otherwise readying them for the coming invasion across the channel from Dover.

Despite all the little things that the Allies did to make sure that QUICKSILVER III was a success, they overlooked one problem with the Bigbobs, as the large inflatable landing craft had been nicknamed. They were too large and too light to withstand the winds that frequently battered the English coast on the edge of the North Sea. This egregious error led one historian to call QUICKSILVER III "an elaborate failure." The same type of decoy landing craft had been used the previous year in Exercise Harlequin, with most of the crafts destroyed or blown ashore. Many of the Bigbobs of Quicksilver III suffered the same fate. Despite being moored to a three-thousand-pound concrete block, many Bigbobs flipped over or were blown ashore, suffering significant damage. Another difficulty was that was that there weren't enough ships to tow the Bigbobs into place. Yet despite these shortcomings and problems with QUICKSILVER III, the "transparent fiction was kept up to the bitter end," with men living at the site to maintain the appearance of activity during the day.

QUICKSILVER IV was different from the other deception operations of FORTITUDE. For one thing, it was not a wholly new operation but rather one that called for an adjustment of bombing runs already being made by the U.S. air forces. This *was* a deception, but of a different sort. The bombs that were dropped by U.S. Army planes were real, but it was *where* they were dropped that formed the deception.

In QUICKSILVER IV, the real operations of the Allied air forces were "adjusted to focus attention on a false objective." While forty-nine German airfields within 150 miles of Caen, near the site of the real invasion, were bombed, only four of the sites were in the NEPTUNE area. On the other hand, eleven were near Pas-de-Calais. In addition, nineteen railroad junctions in the Pas-de-Calais area were bombed. Such bombing included major road and railroad bridges over the rivers Oise and Meuse in northern France. These targets were in support of the real invasion site, but, at the same time, the bombing "drew attention to Pas-de-Calais by severing communications which appeared to lead in that direction." In total, Allied bombers made "twice as many visits to coast defenses and radar stations in the [Pas-de-Calais] area as in the target area."

All this bombing was meant to look like a softening-up operation to make resistance to an invasion more difficult. A secondary aim, however, was to protect the NEPTUNE forces. By taking out road bridges and railroad bridges, the Allies hoped to make it more difficult for German units in the area to speed to Normandy and send supplies, if so ordered.

The Joint Command's plan for QUICKSILVER V called for "special work [to be] carried out to give the impression of extra tunneling" in the famous White Cliffs of Dover. The plan directed that "appropriate new wireless units will be opened up." QUICKSILVER V also called for night lighting at certain places in the area where the dummy landing craft were moored.

Still, the LCS wasn't satisfied with the fake army and fake ships. Reasoning that an army with thousands of vehicles and landing ships needed fuel, the *camoufleurs* constructed a fake oil dock from camouflage-painted boards, sewage pipes, and fiberboard. To make the oil dock seem authentic, King George VI even visited the site, an event that was "leaked" to the press and surely made its way across the channel to the Nazis. The RAF maintained a fighter group in the air to "protect" the facility. To complete the scene, "workers on the ground burned smudge pots filled with crude oil to keep the facility in a haze." And because Dover was in range of Luftwaffe bombers and German heavy guns at Cape Gris Nez, the Allies set fires to convince the Nazis with black smoke that some of their shells had hit home.

QUICKSILVER VI was another physical deception, in this case involving decoy lighting along the south coast of England. The purpose of such fakery was twofold: to convince the Nazis of the authenticity of the FUSAG's buildup, and to divert Nazi attention from the staging areas for NEPTUNE. Although the decoy lighting schemes were elaborate and well planned, they had an unfortunately low impact on the strategy or actions of the Germans. Thaddeus Holt believes that the British Admiralty was "unconscionably slow" in deciding what type of light would be used at the genuine embarkation points. Additionally, the Germans made very little effort at aerial reconnaissance in this area. Of course, the Allies had to plan as if the Nazis would fill the skies with reconnaissance aircraft.

The decoy lighting plan aimed to accomplish different things in two areas of the English coast. First of all, the lighting in the east was meant to be more evidence for the Germans of the troop buildup for an invasion at Pas-de-Calais originating in Dover. The fake lighting in the west, however, was to serve as a decoy to divert Luftwaffe bombers from the troops and the vehicles in the true embarkation area. There were about sixty-five deceptive lighting arrangements: a dozen or so to protect legitimate embarkation points and a similar number to protect ports. In addition, thirty decoy lighting deceptions were established along the southeast coast, with a dozen confusing displays farther down the southern coast.

To support the light shows, recordings were made of the sounds of aircraft roaring down a runway before lifting into the sky. In one such elaborate light-and-sound deception scheme, car headlights were fastened to carts that were "run up and down fake runways at night to simulate planes taking off and landing." In addition, special lights called Q-lights were used to line these fake runways, which, during daylight, were lined with "real looking planes made of nothing but canvas and tubing."

In another type of light deception near the town of

Menabilly, at the very western tip of England, a valley was dammed and flooded. Lights were set up in a way that made it look like Fowey Harbor, which was filled with real landing craft that were destined for use in NEPTUNE. That harbor was kept as dark as possible in the hope that any Luftwaffe bombers that might elude the RAF would drop their bombs in the false Fowey Harbor.

When the real invasion was launched, the work of the British deceivers and the Twenty Committee was hardly finished. Despite the fact that FORTITUDE had indeed caught the Nazis off guard, General Eisenhower needed Hitler's troops and tank corps to remain in Pas-de-Calais for a few more days. He knew that every hour the deception held the Nazis in place would be measured in lives saved. Should the deception fail, the "butcher's bill would soar." And an important component of that deception was the work of the Twenty Committee.

The final chapter of the invasion would not be written until the Allied troops secured the beach and pushed on deep into France. To support that effort, the Twenty Committee needed the Nazi high command to maintain its trust in its agents. The committee and Allied military leaders had gambled on a bold move: they would have a double agent tell the Nazis the time and place of the Normandy landing. The idea wasn't as crazy as it sounds. What better way was there to prove the value of an agent—in this case, Garbo—than to have him deliver that crucial intelligence to the Germans? The information would simply be sent at a time when it would be too late for the Nazis to act on it, yet timely enough to show them that their star agent had delivered the goods.

Timing was the key to this move. Allied troops would hit the beach at 6:30 a.m. on Tuesday, June 6, 1944. Garbo routinely sent messages to a wireless operator in Madrid, who forwarded them to Germany. The Twenty Committee knew that it took three hours for a message to reach Berlin. They decided that Garbo would send his report with details of the Normandy invasion at 3:00 a.m. Garbo made sure that the Madrid wireless operator would be ready to take a message. At the appointed hour, Thomas Robertson of B1A told Sergeant Charles Haines, Garbo's wireless operator, "All right, Sergeant, let them have it!"

Haines might have been nervous, keying such crucial information to the Nazis. However, any nervousness must have been quickly multiplied when the Madrid agent did not respond. That had never happened before. It was perplexing. Was he away from his station, even after being alerted that a message would be coming at this hour? Had he simply fallen asleep? Haines tried again fifteen minutes later. Same result. He kept trying and kept receiving the same response: silence. In the meantime, the message was adjusted to make Garbo's information seem more urgent. Finally, at 8:00 a.m., five hours after the initial attempt to tell the Nazi high command about the invasion of France, the Madrid operator returned to his post and received the message from Garbo. By this time, the Canadian Third Division was charging up the Normandy beaches.

With the invasion under way, it could seem superfluous for the Twenty Committee to persist in having Garbo send his message. The fact that his transmission was received so long after his wireless operator had first tried to send it only added more credibility to Garbo. It appeared that he had tried desperately to send his intelligence, but the Germans had not been prepared to receive it. To emphasize the efforts he had made to forward D-day intelligence, Garbo sent a blistering message to his German handler—a "verbal flamethrower"—taking him to task for missing such critical intelligence.

The committee was not finished with bold moves. More work needed to be done to keep some of Hitler's best troops and tanks near Pas-de-Calais. Garbo's correct warning of the invasion that they saw unfolding in France allowed the Twenty Committee to take advantage of the even stronger trust Hitler had in the double agent. So it was that early on June 9, Garbo sent a message that many World War II historians believe directly induced the Nazis to hold fast to the deception of Pas-de-Calais, thereby sealing the fate of the German army.

Garbo's transmission read, in part:

After personal consultation on 8th June with my agents . . . I am of the opinion, in view of the strong troop concentrations in S.E. and E. England which are not taking part in the present operations, that these operations [in Normandy] are a diversionary maneuver designed to draw off enemy reserves in order then to make a decisive attack in another place. It may probably take place in the Pas-de-Calais area, particularly since in such an attack the proximity of the air bases will facilitate the operation by providing continued strong air support. . . . The constant aerial bombardment which the area of the Pas-de-Calais has suffered and the strategic disposition of these forces give reason to suspect an attack in that region of France which at the same time offers the shortest route for the final objective of their illusions, which is to say Berlin.

His message reinforced all the preconceived notions of the Nazis, especially Hitler, who had believed from the start that Pas-de-Calais was the most logical place for an invasion. In fact, at least as early as March 1943, Hitler believed that it was there, "unless all the indications are misleading—that the decisive battle against the landing forces will be fought." Garbo went on to urge his handler to "submit urgently all these reports and studies to our High Command since moments may be decisive in these times." His handler followed the double agent's suggestion, and the report "hurtled up the chain of command" until it reached Hitler's desk.

For *seven weeks* after the invasion at Normandy, twenty-two divisions of German soldiers (between two hundred fifty thousand and three hundred thousand men), plus their armored equipment, remained near Pas-de-Calais. A handful of divisions were released from the area and moved south toward Normandy. But the reinforcements were meager and their arrival far too late to be of any help. The Allies had not yet won the war, but the Nazis, caught between the Allies in the west and the Russians in the east, had lost it, even though they continued to fight for nearly another year.

The Germans did not realize that they had been so thoroughly deceived. They had such faith in their agent that when Garbo told them at the end of August—nearly eight weeks after D-day—that the FUSAG invasion of Pas-de-Calais had been canceled, the Nazis believed him, as they had believed him all along.

Most historians agree that FORTITUDE was an extraordinary accomplishment that played an integral part in the success of the Normandy invasion. They also agree that certain aspects of the deception were more successful than others. For example, despite great pains taken by the LCS in planning the elaborate wireless deceptions of FORTITUDE, an examination of Y Service files after the war revealed only two instances in which the reports of the double agents were confirmed by a fake wireless intercept.

The Nazis had relied unfailingly on the reports of their spies in England, the very spies who were continually feeding misleading and false intelligence to their handlers. Part of this reliance can be attributed to the handlers themselves, who invested a lot of their own credibility in the spies that they sponsored. Even if the reports seemed a little fishy at times, the German handlers were reluctant to call their own agents (and by association themselves) into question.

Major Hesketh believed that there is only one method of deception that "combines the qualities of precision, certainty, and speed necessary for the conduct of strategic deception at long range and over an extended period": the double agent. In a sense, every other means of deception is something of an insurance policy that supports special means reports. For example, the Luftwaffe may sneak past RAF fighters and catch a glimpse of dummy planes and buildings at an airfield in Scotland, but what can such information mean? However, when a double agent reports that the Allies are preparing to invade Norway and then the reconnaissance planes spot fake planes lining the airfield, such sightings confirm the intelligence supplied by the double agents.

The other means of deception leave too much to chance and misinterpretation. While they may fool the enemy, they, on their own, cannot be counted on to be essential to the success of an operation, especially one of the enormity of FORTITUDE. Such means of deception must always be part of a more comprehensive operation. Hesketh believed that even though FORTITUDE might have succeeded if there had been "no physical deception at all, it would be unwise to assume that such devices can be dispensed with." The Allies had no idea that the Nazis would rely so much on spies, to the near exclusion of other means of intelligence gathering. The spies of the Twenty Committee bamboozled German intelligence on a grand scale, assuring the success of FORTITUDE.

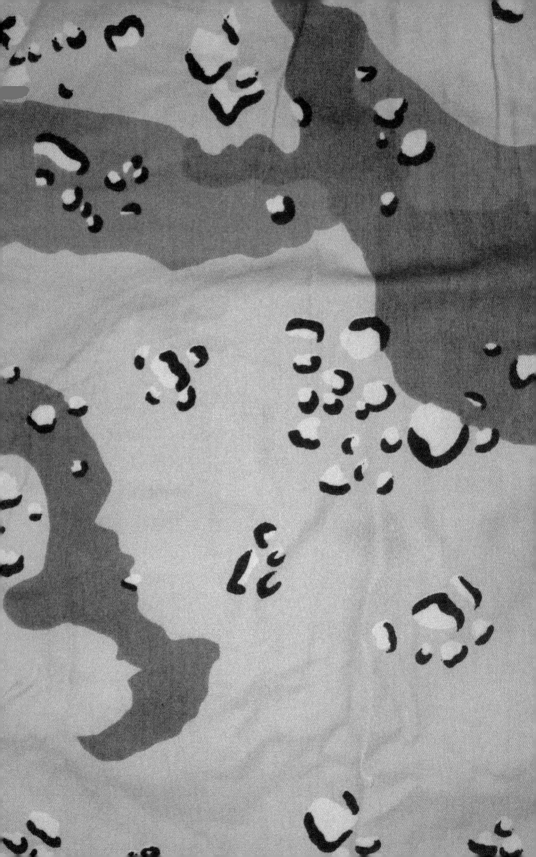

CHAPTER 7

DECEPTION AFTER WORLD WAR II

Almost immediately after World War II, the United States and the Soviet Union, who had been allies against the Nazis, became antagonists in the Cold War, a war of threats and counterthreats with nuclear missiles at the ready. Various flash points around the world intensified the dangerous rivalry between the two superpowers. The war of words between the proponents of democracy and Communism raged for more than forty years, yet without the two powers directly engaging in a shooting war.

The proliferation of nuclear weapons around the globe seemed to signal a shift in the philosophy of the Pentagon and the intelligence community. Following World War II, the U.S. military put more stock in the use of overwhelming firepower to defeat an enemy, backing away from deception operations like the ones that had played a role in the European theater. Some military planners felt that deception was underhanded. So it was that in two of the major wars in which the U.S. became involved after 1950—Korea and Vietnam—the role of deception was greatly diminished. In the Gulf War, however, deception played a more prominent role.

Some of the major differences between World War II and the wars that followed are the scope of combat deaths, geography, and the number of countries involved in warfare. The U.S. soldiers killed in World War II numbered 292,000, or more than three times the number of U.S. combat deaths (about 85,000) in Korea, Vietnam, and Iraq *combined*. Geographically, World War II involved all of Europe, Russia, parts of Africa, and the Middle East, as well as Japan, other islands in the Pacific, and parts of Southeast Asia. By contrast, each of the three wars discussed in this chapter was fought on the soil of relatively small countries.

Another big change was technological, as new weapons were developed. The war in the Pacific ended, after all, when the U.S. dropped atomic bombs on Hiroshima and Nagasaki. Even though later wars were fought in much smaller geographic areas, the players knew that they could unleash mass destruction on the enemy to achieve victory. Strategists believed that there was no need to fool the enemy with deception when they could overpower him with superior weaponry. The success of this philosophy is debatable.

$\bullet$ $\bullet$ $\bullet$

It didn't take long after the signing of the peace treaty that ended World War II for another war to begin. In fact, it had its origins in that very peace treaty between the U.S. and Japan. Japan lost possession of Korea, which had been its protectorate for nearly forty years. Under the terms of the treaty, the United States and the Soviet Union moved troops into Korea and were ready to serve as temporary trustees of the country and to help both the north and south establish free and fair elections. That goal was never reached, leaving Korea divided at the 38th parallel (or latitude 38 degrees north).

North Korea, under a Communist regime, became the Democratic People's Republic of Korea (DPRK). South Korea had an anti-Communist government and became the Republic of Korea (ROK). With no hope of peaceful reunification, the division of the country set the stage for the invasion of South Korea by DPRK troops on June 25, 1950. The Communists were willing, even eager, to use force to unite Korea under their regime.

The invasion, called the "first military action of the Cold War" by some military historians, caught the United States "utterly unprepared." As the North Korean People's Army (KPA) raced down the Korean peninsula, their commanders hoped that a fast conquest of Seoul, the southern capital, would lead to an equally fast surrender by the ROK government. However, the new government was not ready to quit. Its forces, though disorganized, retreated south in the hope that they could hold on until the UN and U.S. sent reinforcements.

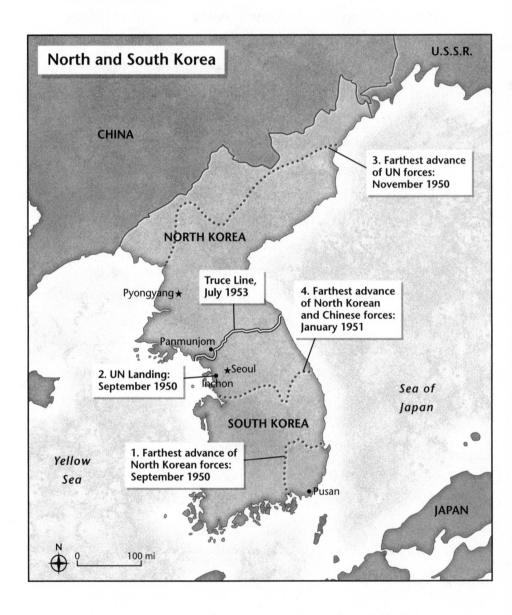

North and South Korea

U.S.S.R.

CHINA

3. Farthest advance of UN forces: November 1950

NORTH KOREA

Pyongyang ★

Truce Line, July 1953

4. Farthest advance of North Korean and Chinese forces: January 1951

Panmunjom •

2. UN Landing: September 1950

★Seoul
Inchon •

Sea of Japan

SOUTH KOREA

1. Farthest advance of North Korean forces: September 1950

Yellow Sea

• Pusan

JAPAN

N
0   100 mi

For nearly eight weeks in the summer of 1950, the campaign raged near Pusan, along the Kum River in the southern tip of South Korea, where U.S. soldiers of the Eighth Army battled alongside South Koreans. The soldiers of the Eighth Army were a small contingent that had remained in the country when most of the U.S. and Soviet troops were pulled out in 1949.

As news of the fall of Seoul reached Washington, officials feared that they were watching the first step of the so-called domino theory—that is, the belief that if one country in Southeast Asia fell to Communism, it was only a matter of time before a neighboring country suffered the same fate. Before long, or so the theory went, the entire region neighboring China and the Soviet Union, the two Communist giants, would form a Communist juggernaut. In the eyes of the U.S., the North Koreans needed to be stopped before the situation got worse.

The U.S. went full speed ahead, getting the United Nations Security Council to agree to send military assistance to the ROK to restore international peace. President Harry Truman, who had become president when Franklin D. Roosevelt died in office on April 12, 1945, invoked the 1947 Truman Doctrine, which stated that the U.S. government would furnish support in the form of economic and military aid to any country or people threatened by Communism or a similar totalitarian ideology. Truman turned to this doctrine in 1950 when he moved quickly to send U.S. troops to Korea as part of a UN force.

On June 25, 1950, the United Nations Security Council passed Resolution 82, condemning the North Korean invasion of the Republic of Korea. Two days later, President Truman agreed to commit two divisions (thirty thousand to forty thousand troops) to General Douglas MacArthur, the commander in chief of the U.S. armed forces in the Far East.

By September, some troops were diverted from Pusan to an area closer to Inchon, on the west coast of Korea, about twenty miles southwest of Seoul. Others were added to the assault force that MacArthur planned to bring ashore at Inchon. MacArthur called the amphibious attack Operation CHROMITE. His navy and marine commanders didn't share his enthusiasm for the invasion. They were opposed to an amphibious invasion behind enemy lines. In addition, they thought that the point of invasion MacArthur had chosen was fraught with danger. A "notoriously self-centered" man, MacArthur ultimately convinced the Joint Chiefs of Staff that the invasion at Inchon was a bold but worthwhile move. He said that he would "rely upon strategic maneuver to overcome the great odds against [him]."

In a cable to the Joint Chiefs of Staff, MacArthur wrote, "The very arguments you have made as to the impracticabilities [sic] involved will tend to ensure me the element of surprise. For the enemy commander will reason that no

General Douglas MacArthur meets with his commander in chief, President Harry Truman.

one would be so brash to make such an attempt." No one, of course, but General Douglas MacArthur. He turned out to be right. The KPA generals believed that Inchon was not a suitable spot for an amphibious landing and that UN forces would choose to attack head-on to drive the KPA troops back up the peninsula to their homeland. Beyond that, the North

Korean commanders never expected the U.S. forces to land behind enemy lines, but that was a critical part of the deception of CHROMITE.

MacArthur planned to gain time by using the troops in the southern tip of the country as a lure to draw the enemy army into a traditional battle line. By drawing the KPA forces so far from home, he was stretching their supply lines, making them more difficult to maintain. At the same time, it was making the North Korean army more vulnerable to a surprise attack. Finally, while the KPA troops were extended far from North Korea, the South Korean and U.S. troops were able to fortify their own positions.

After all the work and worry that went into the landing of U.S. marines at Inchon on September 15, 1950, the event itself seemed "almost anticlimactic." A firm "believer in reconnaissance," MacArthur saw his intelligence proved accurate. The city was "only lightly defended." By 1:30 on the morning of September 16, all the objectives of the mission had been accomplished. U.S. marines joined up with Korean soldiers after capturing Kimpo airfield and marched on Seoul. By the end of September 26, Seoul was liberated. The first phase of MacArthur's plan was a success, due in some measure to the deception that he had pulled off.

Chasing the KPA troops out of South Korea was never MacArthur's sole aim in Korea. When he said prior to the assault, "We shall land at Inchon and I shall crush" the KPA army, he meant to liberate North Korea from Communism as well, and he was not going to let the 38th parallel stop him. So he began the push north. By the middle of November, his forces occupied most of North Korea, including the capital, Pyongyang. MacArthur was determined to press on all the way to the Yalu River, at the Chinese border. What he didn't plan on was the intervention of the disciplined and highly skilled Chinese army, which, he was to learn, was adept at its own brand of deception.

U.S. troops defend a position in South Korea.

As MacArthur and the UN troops pushed closer to the Yalu, Chinese officials were quick to condemn the actions of the UN. Chou En-lai, the foreign minister, declared that the Chinese people "absolutely will not tolerate foreign aggression, nor will they . . . tolerate seeing their neighbors being savagely invaded by imperialists." Chinese General Nieh Jung-chen said that China would not "sit back with folded hands and let the Americans come to the border."

General MacArthur and President Truman, as well as their advisors, were not deterred by China's ominous language. Truman called their words "a bald attempt to blackmail the United Nations." He felt safe minimizing the saber rattling by the Chinese because he believed that the Chinese People's Liberation Army (PLA) did not pose much of a threat to the UN forces. After all, the PLA had no tanks or heavy artillery in its arsenal. Nor did it have an air force or the atomic bomb. It simply was not capable of mounting a war effort that coordinated operations on land and sea and in the air. In addition, the CIA issued nine intelligence reports noting that while it was *possible* the Chinese would intervene in Korea, the idea was considered unlikely.

But General MacArthur was not the only bold strategist at work. The Chinese counterattack began with a deception. The PLA had already massed five hundred thousand troops along the Yalu River, preparing to move into North Korea. Then, around the time of the Inchon invasion, the Chinese troops made their way across the border. They moved at night to prevent detection by UN reconnaissance aircraft. Because the army didn't have a lot of trucks or tanks, the reconnaissance flights didn't observe any change in traffic below the Yalu. Without trucks, the soldiers could keep on the move without using the roads or being burdened with equipment. In this way, "nearly half a million Chinese troops literally sneaked into North Korea."

One army marched three hundred miles from Antung, in Manchuria, to its assembly point in North Korea, serving as a template for the deception plan that the Chinese used. The troops marched at night for eighteen nights, departing no earlier than nine o'clock each night and marching until just before daybreak. At dawn, "every man, every gun, every animal was hidden from sight. In the deep valleys, in thick forests, in the miserable villages huddled on the forlorn plateaus, the Chinese rested by day." Their reaction was clear and disciplined whenever a UN jet approached. Each soldier "was under orders to halt, freezing in his tracks, until the noise of the engines went away." UN aircraft flew over the Chinese troops "hundreds of times without ever once seeing anything suspicious."

Some Chinese troops were actually captured. But MacArthur and his commanders refused to believe that the Chinese were crossing the border in such strong numbers to aid the North Koreans. Surely the reconnaissance flights would have spotted this. MacArthur was quick to accept other explanations for the captured Chinese troops, such as that the Chinese had only sent in a single battalion of troops (three hundred to one thousand men). Such an attitude was "self-deception of the highest order." And it was this same self-deception that made MacArthur and the UN commanders vulnerable to Chinese deceptions, infrequent though they had been to that point. Like any good subterfuge, the Chinese plans were executed with perfect timing in the conflict.

While MacArthur's arrogance led him to belittle the Chinese—they would "never be foolish enough to take on the enormous firepower of a Western mechanized army"—it simultaneously blinded him to the tactics of deception that the Chinese military might use—tactics that the Chinese had, in fact, used in an earlier war with Japan.

As the Chinese soldiers crossed the border into North Korea, they hid during the day in forests, caves, and tunnels dug into the rough terrain of the mountains, their own camouflage matching the "prevailing color of the Korean environment—brown hills, brown villages," making them hard to spot by most reconnaissance planes. The Chinese forces cut off wireless radio communications, making them impossible for the U.S. surveillance units to detect. The Chinese soldiers also used a more drastic method of covering their movements by setting forest fires in North Korea whenever they had to move during the day. The smoke would create a barrier that U.S. planes couldn't see through. The leaders were "well aware of the capabilities and limits of American intelligence." They knew that the U.S. relied on its air force to gather intelligence. And one historian has noted how the Chinese, using the deception technique of false colors, "even marched during daytime, pretending to be [South Korean soldiers], knowing that the airplanes would not be able to tell the difference." Because the Chinese army didn't use "conventional means of detecting modern military movement—wireless traffic, mechanized activity, supply dumps"—the UN command was blind to what was going on right in front of them.

The deception, when realized, was a shock to MacArthur and his commanders. But it paled in comparison to the horrors that the UN troops later suffered in battle against the Chinese troops. Taking a page from the book of historical deceptions, the Chinese planned to trap the UN forces by means of a feint, much like the tactic that Duke William II of Normandy used in the Battle of Hastings in 1066. It worked just as well nearly nine hundred years later against the commander of the UN forces in Korea.

The Chinese went on the offensive on November 1, but only on a small scale as they "wrecked several South Korean regiments and roughed up an American regiment as well." The ambush was meant to push the UN troops south, away from the Yalu. Then, for no apparent reason, the Chinese halted their attack. During the lull in the battle, more Chinese troops crossed the border, but, holding to their tactics, these troops remained hidden. The pause in the fighting lasted for a couple of weeks. While the UN troops rested and resupplied, the Chinese waited. On November 25, the UN troops began a cautious march north, with orders that they were to pull back as soon as they ran into Chinese troops. "This was good advice," one historian believes, "and risky for the careers of the UN commanders who gave it—but it wasn't enough."

Pursuing the Chinese troops in their false retreat proved catastrophic to the UN troops. The enemy attacked in a fury that caught the UN troops in a trap, finding their force half the size of the four hundred thousand Chinese troops sent against them. The UN troops were quickly outflanked by the elusive enemy that gave the impression of "popping out of the hills." The UN tactical strength—relying on trucks and other heavy equipment—proved to be a deadly liability, as they were forced to stick to the roads while the Chinese attacked from all sides, then vanished. When the smoke cleared and the dead and wounded UN soldiers were accounted for, the consequences were clear: the American soldiers had suffered one of their most crushing defeats of the century.

The military setbacks forced President Truman to install new military commanders. In April 1951, he fired General MacArthur for insubordination when the general pushed for the U.S. to use nuclear bombs against China. He was also held accountable for having provoked China at a juncture where a peace settlement might have been possible. MacArthur's successor, General Matthew Ridgway, regrouped and attacked the Chinese army. The Chinese were driven from Seoul and pushed back across the 38th parallel. Even though the enemy armies had been driven from South Korea, the fighting continued along the border.

By July, the U.S. had initiated peace talks with the North Koreans at Panmunjom, even as the fighting continued. Finally, after two years of high-stakes negotiations and bitter fighting, an armistice was signed on July 27, 1953. The peace accord drew a new border near the 38th parallel that gave South Korea an additional fifteen hundred square miles of territory. The peace treaty also created a two-mile-wide "demilitarized zone," a buffer between the two countries that still exists today, complete with observation towers, armed border guards, and a no-man's-land.

Like the conflict that brought U.S. soldiers halfway around the world to Korea in 1950, the Vietnam War involved a small country that had been divided into north and south after another conflict—the First Indochina War. Citing the domino theory, the White House was eager to keep Vietnam from falling into Communist hands. A framework was created for sending military and economic aid to Vietnam.

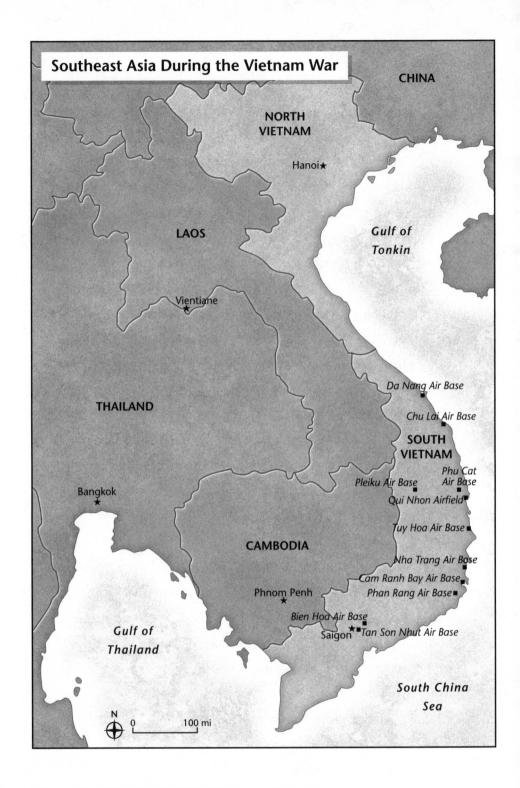

Southeast Asia During the Vietnam War

CHINA

NORTH VIETNAM

Hanoi★

LAOS

Gulf of Tonkin

Vientiane★

THAILAND

Da Nang Air Base ■

Chu Lai Air Base ■

SOUTH VIETNAM

Phu Cat Air Base

Pleiku Air Base ■

Qui Nhon Airfield ■

Bangkok ★

Tuy Hoa Air Base ■

CAMBODIA

Nha Trang Air Base ■

Cam Ranh Bay Air Base ■

Phnom Penh ★

Phan Rang Air Base ■

Bien Hoa Air Base ★

Gulf of Thailand

Saigon ★ ■ Tan Son Nhut Air Base

South China Sea

N

0   100 mi

Another parallel between Korea and Vietnam is apparent in how the U.S. military conducted the war. In both cases, the U.S. relied on massive firepower to subdue the enemy, and such an approach did not deliver victory in either war. There was continued disdain from the U.S. military commanders for deception operations. Although CHROMITE had been successful in the Korean War, it was planned and executed over the strenuous objections of some members of the Joint Chiefs of Staff. The U.S. efforts at organized deception in Vietnam were limited, and the U.S. military did not encourage its Vietnamese partners in the war to try such tactics.

The first shipment of U.S. military aid to the new South Vietnam arrived in the capital, Saigon, early in 1955. In addition, the Pentagon offered to train South Vietnam's army to protect the country from Ho Chi Minh (North Vietnam's head of state) and the People's War to unite North and South Vietnam. In July 1956, the first U.S. military advisors were killed by Viet Minh guerillas.

By 1965, two hundred thousand U.S. troops were fighting in South Vietnam for a government that changed leadership with such disturbing frequency that Maxwell Taylor, the U.S. ambassador to South Vietnam, warned that Americans were "tired of coups."

As the U.S. role in Vietnam deepened, the military relied more and more on dropping bombs on the Viet Cong and on North Vietnam. In fact, the 4.2 million tons of bombs dropped on the enemy by U.S. bombers was about 25 percent

more than the U.S. and Great Britain combined dropped in
World War II. U.S ground forces in Vietnam were strongly
tied to "fire bases," which were generally mountaintop artillery bases "from which a great weight of artillery fire could be
brought to bear anywhere in the area of operations."

U.S. Huey helicopters fly in formation over a landing zone in South Vietnam.

There remained something of a cultural prejudice against deception. Because the Viet Cong "used deception to such good effect," it was considered by some in the Pentagon to be "an enemy tactic . . . un-American." With such a tactical bias, it was no wonder that covert operations and deceptions

did not receive much consideration from the Pentagon. Yet in 1961, President John F. Kennedy tasked the CIA with covert operations in Vietnam.

While there was never a significant coordinated effort by the U.S. for military deception, the Viet Cong were, in the words of an intelligence expert, "masters of subterfuge." They were extremely adept at using ruses against South Vietnamese troops. One of their more common and successful ruses was false colors. Just as the Trojan soldiers put on the battle gear of the fallen Greeks and the Chinese wore the colors of the Koreans, the VC would wear the uniform of the South Vietnam army and attack U.S. bases.

The VC also effectively employed the feint. One variation was to send a small unit of soldiers to attack one of the vulnerable spots in the barbed wire strung around U.S. bases. When the U.S. soldiers responded to such an attack, the main body of VC troops would attack areas of the perimeter that U.S. soldiers had left unprotected. The VC also used a feint in the jungles. A small group of enemy soldiers would attack an American unit on patrol. Knowing that the U.S. would rush reinforcements to the point of attack, the VC waited with their own ambush along the trail they suspected the Americans would use to aid their unit.

The fact that the VC rarely tried to deceive by using demonstration shows how they understood their own strategic strengths and weaknesses as well as those of the U.S. forces. The VC weren't likely to deploy the large number of troops needed to pull off a demonstration. But perhaps a more important reason for not using that technique was the knowledge that the U.S. was capable of raining heavy bombardment on the decoy troops used in a demonstration.

The success of Operation FORTITUDE relied on the tight security that the Allies maintained. That was a far cry from what the U.S. was able to achieve in Vietnam. Any deception plan that the U.S. could have come up with would have soon been compromised by North Vietnamese spies in South Vietnam. The American armed forces installations in Vietnam were riddled with spies and Communist sympathizers. They were so widespread because the Vietnam War was, at its heart, a war among one people over the unification of their country. The U.S. hired "thousands of South Vietnamese to work on the bases and headquarters," and many of these "turned out to be Communist agents or sympathizers."

The U.S. engaged in some minor deceptions, but like those in earlier centuries, they were tactical battlefield deceptions that were limited in scope and mainly the work of individual commanders. For example, the U.S. tried to use the helicopters in its arsenal to its advantage by setting up fake landing zones. The armed forces developed a scheme in which helicopters would make several jungle landings, but leave soldiers and equipment at only one of the drop zones. The U.S. knew that the VC could not investigate all the drops, but by looking for several sites they would thin their numbers, making them more vulnerable to attack.

Another tactic was used by U.S. helicopter gunships to assist landing parties. They "let go with some firepower," thus attracting VC troops. Because the VC generally had no radios as they roamed the jungle, they could not communicate with their comrades. As a result, multiple VC units would probe the source of the gunfire, giving U.S. troops the chance to land in another area.

Deception operations by the U.S. in Vietnam were under the direction of the CIA. William Colby, chief of the CIA's Saigon station and later director of the agency, explained that the purpose of the covert program was to "increase the insecurity in North Vietnam to match the insecurity that they were producing in South Vietnam" and to "establish a base for resistance guerrilla operations." Perhaps such vague expectations can in part explain why the early covert efforts in Vietnam were a fiasco. By 1962 President Kennedy was dissatisfied with the numerous mistakes of the spy agency.

A counterintelligence review revealed that most of the agents sent into North Vietnam "were either captured or doubled [became double agents] sometime shortly after they got there." The review also discovered that many of the radio operators sending messages back to their handlers in South Vietnam had been compromised or were working as double agents. Most damning of all the evidence found in the investigation was the fact that the CIA was never able to safely extricate a team of agents.

Kennedy turned over the deception operations to the

military. Among other things, he charged the military with ratcheting up the size and scope of the covert war. The Pentagon responded with Operational Plan 34A (OPLAN 34A), which consisted of a "total of 72 [categories of] actions . . . [containing] a total of 2,062 separate operations" that were to begin in 1964. OPLAN 34A called for a "major escalation of America's secret war." But having a plan for covert ops is a far cry from having the organizational structure and agents to execute it. OPLAN 34A was a "complex deception program to create the perception of a growing and active underground movement with the objective of forcing the North Vietnam government to withdraw support for the VC."

Even when the military took over covert operations in North Vietnam, it was never really sold on the value of deception. The Pentagon's attitude on such operations remained unchanged. They believed that the path to victory involved dropping thousands of tons of bombs and firing countless artillery shells.

A month after President Kennedy was assassinated, in November 1963, President Lyndon Johnson ordered a thorough study of OPLAN 34A to determine its least risky actions. He wasn't seeking the most effective actions. The following year, the Military Assistance Command, Vietnam (MACV), created a "highly secret new organization to execute these operations." It was called the MACV Studies and Observations Group, or simply the SOG.

A study of all the files from the CIA's attempt to infiltrate

North Vietnam with agents showed how significant a disaster the operations had been. The North Vietnamese were running their own version of the double-cross system that the Allies had used so successfully in World War II. "All the teams that OP 34 assumed were legitimate were actually under the control of Hanoi's Ministry of the Interior." Hanoi (the North Vietnamese capital) even knew about OPLAN 34A's codes and ciphers, and some of the agents had been "run back against first the CIA, and then the SOG."

The only bright light in all this was that the U.S. had discovered the double agents' deception and could do something about it, unlike Hitler, who never knew that the Allies were using his spies against him. The U.S. decided to turn the double-cross system into a triple cross and use it against Ho Chi Minh and Hanoi.

The intelligence that the U.S. military had been able to gather about North Vietnam indicated a country that had become more and more concerned about spies among its population. And, as one intelligence expert has noted, "a fixation on subversion, deception, and conspiracy can take its toll." When he became aware of such intelligence, the chief of the SOG, Major General John Singlaub, believed that OPLAN 34A should be "cranked up and expanded, but with a very different purpose." It was time, he believed, for the SOG "to play hardball."

What Singlaub had in mind was a triple-cross system that would turn the tables on the North Vietnamese and convince them that the agents they had captured and turned into double agents were only a small piece of a much larger and complicated network intent on destabilizing North Vietnam. The U.S. hoped that the North Vietnamese would take the bait and use more resources to pursue these notional spies—resources that could not then be spent on troops.

The diversionary program was approved on March 14, 1968, and was code-named FORAE. It grew from an earlier deception that dropped radios into North Vietnam, some to broadcast "black" radio programs (programs that could not be traced back to the U.S.) and others to receive messages about phony rendezvous points for agents who didn't exist. The goal of the radio deception was to get the North Vietnamese to believe that the radios were meant for spy teams that hadn't been able to pick up their radios before they were discovered. Although it is unlikely that the North Vietnamese were taken in by this scheme, it was a foundation for Operation FORAE.

FORAE included three deception projects: Borden, Urgency, and Oodles. All were designed to take advantage of Hanoi's growing paranoia about spies on the loose in North Vietnam and to "create the impression that an active, unified, internal opposition exist[ed] in North Vietnam."

Project Borden recruited North Vietnamese prisoners of war to work as SOG agents. The POW agents were nothing more than pawns in the SOG's plan. The SOG selected prisoners that it thought would cooperate, although it didn't matter if the POWs told the truth about their interest in becoming agents. What mattered was that they were willing to be trained and returned to North Vietnam.

During the training period, the recruits were allowed to overhear rumors about agents and spy teams already in the field. The rumors could even include tidbits about corrupt government officials. Once back in their part of the country, the "agents" would carry the false information to North Vietnam intelligence interrogators. The SOG thoroughly expected the new agents to spill their "secrets" as soon as they were taken into custody in the north. They would reveal that they were to meet up with (notional) U.S. spies already in the country.

Project Urgency included two operations. The first involved POWs who were uncooperative—the "most zealous Communists." These POWs were taken to Cu Lao Cham, known to the Americans as Paradise Island, fifteen miles off Da Nang in the South China Sea. On the island they were indoctrinated about a notional resistance movement, the Sacred Sword of the Patriots League, which was designed to counter the regime in Hanoi. These "hard cases" were then dropped into North Vietnam. Often, incriminating items were sewn into their clothes without their knowledge. The expectation was that these "agents," too, would be vigorously interrogated when this hidden information was discovered by the North Vietnamese. This operation stoked the fires of suspicion that gripped Hanoi. As one of the U.S. trainers put it, "it was highly likely that the interrogation process would turn ugly [and we] were hoping they'd all be killed or give false information that we planted."

The second operation of Project Urgency, similar to Project Borden, took place on Paradise Island and involved prisoners who wanted to cooperate and work as agents in "a completely scripted . . . affair" in which everything these would-be agents saw, heard, and learned was planted information about the number of agents in the north regularly sending valuable military intelligence. The whole training process ended with an elaborate "special ceremony where the 'new agent' was inducted into a secret brotherhood," which was a perfect bogus ending to the bogus training program. Back in North Vietnam, their purpose was to tell the North Vietnam intelligence agents all the false information they had learned on Paradise Island.

Project Oodles was a more advanced variation of the early radio deception. At the core of the project were fourteen phantom teams of spies "in place" in North Vietnam. False radio messages were sent by OPLAN 34A to each notional team, which included operation directions as well as personal messages from family members, such as birthday or anniversary wishes from a spouse.

To reinforce the belief in these teams, empty resupply bundles were dropped by parachute in an area where a team was supposed to be operating. North Vietnamese soldiers would find the bundles but, of course, not the supplies that were supposed to be in them, giving the impression that they were too late to catch the agents, who had already retrieved the supplies and vanished into the jungle.

Another ploy was to drop blocks of ice in personal parachutes. The chutes would get snagged in the trees and the ice would melt quickly in the jungle heat, leaving only a personal parachute and a clear message to the North Vietnamese soldiers who found them: too late again. Finally, transmitting radios were also dropped. Messages were coming in for the agents, and answers were being transmitted by them. The pseudo-agents created by the U.S. had no idea how they were being manipulated. All these discoveries were unsettling for the North Vietnamese intelligence agency.

After false starts and setbacks, OPLAN 34A seemed to be heading in the right direction by the fall of 1968. The diversionary program "clearly was having the intended effect," even though it was a fledgling operation. Hanoi was "feeling the heat and becoming increasingly sensitive to the threat of subversion." Newspapers and broadcast media in the north "revealed an increasing alarm over agents, spies, and espionage." In addition, the beginning of an intricate triple-cross system was in place. U.S. intelligence agents believed that it would soon bear fruit.

Despite these indications that the deception operations were working, President Johnson ordered an end to all deception ops that called for agents crossing into North Vietnam. In an effort to encourage peace talks and conclude what had become a very long war, the U.S. agreed to halt all acts of war inside North Vietnam—which, of course, included the diversionary program. Barely begun, the deception operations were shut down.

Still the war continued. Although the U.S. began to withdraw troops in 1969 under President Richard Nixon, the process dragged on for nearly four years. The last U.S. ground troops left Vietnam on March 29, 1973. Unlike the Korean War, which ended in a stalemate and a return to the status quo of two independent nations divided by a demilitarized zone, the Vietnam War ended with a unified Vietnam, controlled by a Communist regime.

While the wars in Korea and Vietnam were fought, as the U.S. military believed, to block the spread of Communism and "win the hearts and minds" of the people in countries the U.S. thought it was helping, the Gulf War of 1990–1991 was about something more tangible—essential, in fact, for the world to function: oil. It began after an attempt by Iraq's president, Saddam Hussein, to control a large share of the oil flowing from the Middle East.

Unlike the wars in Korea and Vietnam, deception played a significant part in the war against Iraq. However, the use of overwhelming firepower as the cornerstone of overall strategy did not change. The war began with a prolonged period of aerial bombardment. Nevertheless, the ground war hinged on the use of deception.

There were a number of factors that led the U.S. military to use deception in the Gulf War. First of all, the war involved a relatively small geographic area. Kuwait covers about seven thousand square miles, roughly the size of New Jersey. While the entire war wasn't fought in Kuwait, it was limited to an area around this small country. A related consideration was the fact that the war was fought in a flat and open desert, a far cry from the mountains of Korea or the jungles of Vietnam.

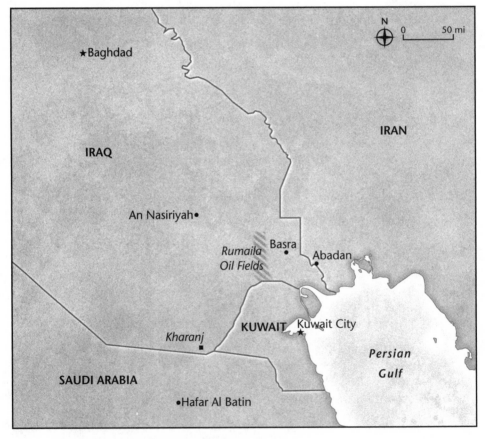

Kuwait and surrounding countries

Further, the U.S. had a firm conviction that, if Coalition troops could neutralize the Iraqi air force and pull off a battlefield deception, they would then have the upper hand in a ground war. The war, the U.S. military reasoned, could conclude in relatively short order, certainly nothing like the three years in Korea or the roughly twenty years in Vietnam. A short war would mean limited casualties. As General Barry McCaffrey said, "The whole notion is to bypass the enemy's strengths and reduce the amount of bloodshed to us and to them."

Finally, advanced technology made it easier for U.S. soldiers to deliver a knockout punch to the Iraqi army. The Global Positioning System (GPS) proved especially critical in pulling off deception in the desert.

When the Iraqis invaded Kuwait in 1990, the U.S. and other world powers were worried that if Saddam Hussein controlled the oil in Kuwait, he might next invade Saudi Arabia, a longtime friend of the U.S. If Saudi Arabia then fell, Iraq would control 20 percent of the world's oil supply. U.S. president George H. W. Bush would not let that stand. In the five years prior to the war, U.S. oil consumption had crept steadily higher, from 15.7 thousand barrels per day to 17.3 thousand barrels per day. The Gulf War began with rhetoric and accusations, and ended with a remarkable one hundred hours of ground combat.

THE GLOBAL POSITIONING SYSTEM

FOR THOUSANDS OF YEARS, sailors found their way over vast seas by using a sextant to measure the angle between the horizon and heavenly bodies like the sun and the moon. Such measures told longitude and latitude, invaluable for determining the position of a ship. In the late twentieth century, these methods changed. Modern sailors use a navigation system that relies on satellites—artificial celestial bodies—to find their way. Navigation satellites launched by the U.S. Air Force circle the globe, sending radio signals that are "translated" by a Global Positioning System (GPS) receiver. GPS receivers are now standard in many handheld devices, like smartphones and tablets, and are included in many car dashboards to help drivers navigate highways and city streets.

Beyond its everyday use, GPS has become the U.S. military's "backbone for its battlefield communications system." Operation DESERT STORM, the second phase of the Gulf War, was the first conflict in which GPS was widely used. During the Gulf War, there was a "maximum of one receiver per company of 180 men." Ten years later, in the Iraq War, there were "more than 100,000 Precision Lightweight GPS Receivers . . . for the land forces and at least one per nine-man squad."

At the time of DESERT STORM, GPS relied on a "constellation" of twenty-seven satellites (twenty-four in operation and three spares) that circled the earth at an elevation of about twelve thousand miles in four evenly spaced orbits, making two complete orbits every day. There are now thirty-two satellites, allowing for even better reception, with six visible at any one time. Each satellite weighs between three thousand and four thousand pounds and orbits the earth at about nine thousand miles per hour, broadcasting a signal with two bits of information: the precise time on its atomic clock and the satellite's exact location. A GPS receiver then uses simultaneous readings from three different satellites to determine its longitude and latitude, or its exact location on the earth. GPS needs to be equipped with mapping software that can read the information from the satellite and plot location and movement.

It was this GPS mapping ability that allowed the troops and equipment of the Coalition forces to move so confidentially without regard to road signs or physical markers. The Iraqis were amazed that the enemy could "own the night" and move through adverse weather conditions, such as sandstorms. The U.S. military found GPS to be a "godsend for ground troops traversing the desert, especially in the frequent sandstorms. . . . Tank crews and drivers of all sorts of vehicles swore by the system." But the usefulness of GPS extended beyond actual combat. Even trucks carrying meals to the troops were GPS-equipped, allowing drivers to "find and feed soldiers of frontline units widely dispersed among the dunes."

Although relations between Iraq and its neighbors ranged between contentious and hostile, as seen in the Iraq-Iran War (1980–1988), most experts look at July 17, 1990, as the first inkling that greater trouble was on the horizon in the oil-rich region. On that day, Saddam Hussein leveled charges against Kuwait that it was overproducing oil, thereby driving down the cost of oil. However, the more serious accusation was that Kuwait, through "slant drilling," was stealing oil from the Iraqi Rumaila oil field, which was located about twenty miles west of Basra and straddled the Iraq-Kuwait border. Rumaila, the largest oil field in Iraq and the fourth largest in the world, was believed to hold seventeen billion barrels of oil.

With hostilities simmering, Saddam Hussein invaded Kuwait on August 2, 1990, with a two-pronged attack. The main force of the Iraqi army drove straight south on the main highway into the capital, Kuwait City. Another Iraqi force took a more westerly route before turning to the east, cutting off the capital from the southern part of the country and acting as something of a barrier between Kuwait City and Saudi Arabia. Within hours, about 20 percent of Kuwait's air force planes were destroyed or captured. By the end of the day, Kuwaiti resistance to the invasion crumbled and the emir and his family fled.

Despite its enormous oil wealth, Kuwait was no military match for the Iraqi army, which included about five thousand tanks and seven thousand military aircraft and helicopters. In addition to the heavy hardware, Saddam Hussein could draw on over a million and a half regular army troops and reservists. Kuwait's army included about fifteen thousand men, half of whom fled to Saudi Arabia shortly after the invasion. Comparisons of their machines of war—tanks, planes, armored troop carriers, artillery—further showed Iraq to have a superior army.

Saddam Hussein got what he wanted: control of the oil fields of Kuwait. He installed a temporary puppet government that he called the Provisional Government of Free Kuwait. Within a week of the invasion, however, in an attempt to give an air of legitimacy to this government, he appointed his cousin Ali Hassan al-Majid as the leader of what Hussein called the Republic of Kuwait.

While the world looked on in shock at Saddam Hussein's attack, the U.S. began to take action. President Bush believed that Saddam Hussein needed to be held accountable for his actions.

As President Truman had done forty years earlier when he saw the Communist threat in Korea, Bush quickly brought the issue to the United Nations, seeking its support through sanctions against Saddam Hussein and his regime. The UN acted with a sense of urgency, issuing UN Resolution 600, which condemned the Iraqi invasion and demanded a withdrawal of all Iraqi troops from Kuwait. Other resolutions soon followed until Saddam Hussein was ready to compromise. The U.S., however, refused to negotiate with him until the Iraqi forces left Kuwait—and that wasn't in Hussein's plans.

The UN issued twelve resolutions condemning the actions of Iraq. Finally, at the end of November, the UN issued Resolution 678, which gave Hussein until January 15, 1991, to remove all his troops from Kuwait. The resolution authorized the use of "all necessary means" by the coalition of nations against the Iraqi occupation of Kuwait if Iraq did not withdraw by the deadline.

While they waited, in an attempt to turn world sentiment against Saddam Hussein and his invading army, the U.S. formalized a coalition of nations that were willing to take a stand against Iraq and come to the aid of Kuwait. More than thirty countries pledged personnel and/or funding—more than $53 billion—for the Coalition army, which would be commanded by General Norman Schwarzkopf. About 70 percent of the nearly one million troops came from the U.S.

King Fahd of Saudi Arabia asked for U.S. troops to protect his country from aggression by Iraq. The U.S. promptly agreed, and the new deployment of nearly 500,000 troops was called Operation DESERT SHIELD. The buildup of troops continued into the new year. As the role of the U.S. in the area changed from defending Saudi Arabia to preparing to oust Saddam Hussein from Kuwait, so did the name of the mission. It was now called Operation DESERT STORM.

As January 15, 1991—the deadline set by the UN for withdrawal of Iraqi troops from Kuwait—dawned in the desert, the Iraqi army held its positions. The following evening at about 6:30 EST (early in the morning of January 17 in

U.S. General Norman Schwarzkopf, commander of Coalition forces

Kuwait), DESERT STORM began. The first phase of the operation called for five weeks of relentless aerial pounding by Coalition bombers. The U.S., with nearly 1,800 planes nearby on land and on aircraft carriers in the Persian Gulf, flew most of the missions. Their sorties, augmented by British, French, and Saudi Arabian jets, were meant to destroy the Iraqi air force and cripple Saddam Hussein's ability to obtain valuable intelligence from the air. The air war was successful in "blinding" the Iraqi air force and preparing the way for the ground war and the deceptions that were to follow.

The ground war was planned to last exactly one hundred hours under the leadership of General Schwarzkopf. From the very beginning of planning for the ground war, the Coalition strategy was based on a deception. As with other successful deceptions, like FORTITUDE SOUTH, the enemy had to be distracted from the real point of attack and commit his troops to the *apparent* point of attack. To accomplish this, the Coalition planners needed to take advantage of Saddam Hussein's preconceptions, just as the Allies had taken advantage of Hitler's preconceptions before the D-day invasion at Normandy.

The most important preconception that Saddam Hussein held was that the Coalition army would certainly attack from Saudi Arabia. In fact, early intelligence indicated to Hussein that the attack would come from an area near Wadi Al Batin — *wadi* is the Arabic word for "valley" or "dry riverbed" — which ran along the western border of Iraq and Kuwait into Saudi Arabia.

To support this notion, CNN and print reporters in the press pool that were covering the impending ground war were allowed to report from the area about the maneuvers of the Coalition army. The reporters, however, were not allowed access to the U.S. troops that were leaving the area to form the "left hook" of the deception. As a security measure, the units remaining in the staging area sent false radio signals that were meant to be coming from the XVIII Corps, which in reality had left to play its part in an upcoming tactical deception.

Unaware they were playing a part in the demonstration, the news organizations covered the exercises of the U.S. Marine Expeditionary Forces that were taking part in an amphibious training exercise off the Kuwaiti coast. These exercises included an operation called IMMINENT THUNDER, a five-day land and air training exercise, which included mock bombing raids by Kuwaiti pilots to show that they could provide air support for Coalition ground forces. In addition, a U.S. Navy SEAL task force conducted "an amphibious feint, supported by naval gunfire, to reinforce the threat" of troops storming the beaches. Such televised reports, seen by Saddam Hussein and his advisors, "precisely reinforced the deceptive scheme" that the Coalition forces would attack by sea.

The demonstration of an amphibious attack led Hussein to shift some of his troops from the area of the Kuwait–Saudi Arabia border to the coast. Consequently, the Coalition troops along the border near Wadi Al Batin "faced units at only 50 to 75% of their original strength," even as the Iraqis still expected an attack on the Kuwaiti southern border.

The first pieces of the deception were in place. The Iraqi troops along the border with Saudi Arabia were hunkered down, but some had withdrawn and moved east to the coast to repel an amphibious landing. The final piece of the operation would stop supplies and reinforcements from moving south from Iraq to help the troops already in Kuwait. General Schwarzkopf knew that the "dug-in Iraqis were essentially immobilized along the Kuwaiti border" and at the Persian Gulf.

It was time to launch the final phase of the deception: what Schwarzkopf called his Hail Mary play, a reference to a football strategy in which the team with the ball goes for broke in an attempt to win the game. The general's Hail Mary play was to move a "huge mass of 20,000 vehicles . . . at a rate of over 100 miles a day for nearly a week" into the Iraqi desert north of Kuwait, knowing that the Iraqi troops were not about to move from the southern border of Kuwait, from Wadi Al Batin to the Persian Gulf. The Iraqi commanders would never expect the Coalition troops to come roaring across the "western wastelands" of Iraq.

In the final analysis, there were a number of reasons why Saddam Hussein fell for the deception, and they were all driven by what U.S. intelligence agencies knew were his preconceptions about the U.S. troops and their involvement in the war. First, Saddam Hussein believed that American voters and politicians would not support another war. They remembered too well, he believed, the blunders and the body bags of the Vietnam War. He gambled that the U.S. would not attack outright for fear that casualties would not play well back home. He was, in a sense, calling the bluff of the U.S.

The second preconception involved the desert. Even though Iraq is 40 percent desert, the Iraqis themselves "were not used to operating in the desert," which many considered to be a perilous place and "had regarded it as such for thousands of years." A related miscalculation was the Iraqi belief that even the GPS installed in Coalition tanks and rolling equipment would not help the Coalition troops to cross such a wide expanse of desert. Saddam Hussein and Iraqi commanders didn't yet realize how the GPS "would revolutionize desert navigation." Instead of relying on aerial reconnaissance, an army could, in a sense, let the GPS be its eyes. The Coalition tanks could operate without reference to landmarks. Their sophisticated GPS devices allowed them to lock in on a target and attack without wasting time trying to find the enemy.

A report by the Naval War College, "Deception in Operations Desert Shield/Desert Storm," found that the Iraqis "considered armor movement to the west of their positions in Kuwait infeasible as their own experience in training . . . resulted in complete lack of operational integration and attendant navigational problems." In fact, in such desert exercises, the Iraqis had often gotten lost and were "incapable of massing combat power in terrain without features." By the time the war ended, however, the Iraqis had learned about the effectiveness of GPS. They were also mistaken in another preconception: that the Coalition troops would not cross the border into Iraq. It was another lesson learned too late.

The intelligence community generally believes that maintaining deception becomes more difficult as the number of intelligence-gathering channels available to an enemy increases. However, "within limits, the greater the number of controlled channels, the greater the likelihood of the deception being believed." Because the Iraqis had few ways to gather intelligence, the chances of the success of the ground plan deception were increased. Just as with FORTITUDE SOUTH, one of the keys to the success of the Coalition deception was controlling the intelligence that Saddam Hussein received. That meant controlling the television and radio news channels.

The Coalition was able to control TV and radio transmissions to advance the deception plans. To emphasize the deception of the coastal attack, CNN reported on offshore maneuvers, but was kept in the dark about the troops that were not where Hussein thought they were. Because Iraq was still able to monitor Coalition wireless transmissions, they were a good channel to convey misinformation to the Iraqis. For example, when Coalition units that had been at the wadi left to participate in the Hail Mary deception, remnants of the units remained behind to send bogus radio messages to give the impression that the soldiers at the wadi were at full strength.

On Sunday morning, February 24, 1991, the first and second marine divisions and Saudi troops launched a feint attack through the wadi and met "little resistance" because many of the Iraqi troops had been moved to protect Kuwait City. Troops of the Marine Expeditionary Force had a similar experience when they crossed into Kuwait near the coast. Iraqi forces fell back so quickly that Schwarzkopf had to begin the Hail Mary deception eighteen hours earlier than he had planned.

The hasty change in plans could only be achieved because of the precise planning of the sequence of events. Even though DESERT STORM was a more modest operation than FORTITUDE SOUTH, the sequencing of all its parts was crucial to success. The commanders of the different components of the deception needed to be in constant communication with one another to make sure that the parts of the deception left no gaps that might throw suspicion on the operation. The importance of "each commander being aware of the intent and importance of the deception plan cannot be overlooked," as Daniel L. Breitenbach wrote of the Naval War College.

The U.S. military was able to apply what it knew

about the tendencies of the Iraqi troops against them on the battlefield. Following eight years of fighting the Iranians, the Iraqi army remained very defense-minded, which caused them to set up "an impressive-looking line of defenses along the Kuwait–Saudi Arabia border." They also showed a preference for large armored ambushes, in which they often utilized the same deception strategy that the Chinese army used in the Korean War against U.S. and UN troops. Specifically, when an enemy attacked, the Iraqis retreated and allowed the enemy army to pursue them until they were in a position where hidden Iraqi forces could attack the flanks of their enemy. In this war, the Iraqis wanted the Coalition forces to "attack into the teeth of the defense" and the Coalition "gave them what they wanted" by confronting the Iraqis at the wadi and near the gulf and letting them think that the Coalition forces were going to engage in a frontal attack.

Troops in both operations marched on Kuwait City. In the meantime, the Hail Mary was in full operation to the west, on the left flank of the Coalition attack. A French light armored unit, operating in conjunction with the U.S. Eighty-Second Airborne, sped north to within 150 miles of Baghdad. Their job was to block any reinforcements that Saddam Hussein might try to send south. To their right, the U.S. Eighteenth Airborne moved far into Iraq, then made a dramatic turn to the east, attacking Basra. To their right, the U.S Seventh Armored Corps operating with the British First Armored

Division also turned east to engage in a major tank battle with the elite Iraqi Republican Guard. Slowly, the Coalition troops were blocking reinforcements moving south and retreating troops fleeing north.

Fighting continued on February 25 and 26, with various groups of Coalition troops playing their part in sealing off northern positions. All the while, the Saudis and U.S. marines closed in on Kuwait City from the south. By February 27, the U.S. Eighteenth Airborne had created "a solid wall across the north," while fighting the Republican Guard to the east. In the meantime, the U.S. First Marines controlled the airport. Finally, the Second Marines blocked any escape routes out of the capital. In the words of General Schwarzkopf, "The gates are closed."

On February 28, at 8 a.m. in the Middle East, President Bush ordered an end to offensive operations in Kuwait and Iraq. The hundred-hour war had been won. Coalition forces were credited with destroying or damaging nearly eleven hundred tanks, about six hundred military pieces, and a number of anti-aircraft guided missile launchers. They captured more than twenty thousand Iraqi soldiers.

There are a number of ways to measure the success of deceptive measures associated with Operations DESERT SHIELD and DESERT STORM. A report by the Naval War College noted that the deceptions may have had little impact on the military outcome of the war. The Coalition forces were, after all, clearly superior to the forces of Hussein in equipment, training, and leadership. The report went on to say, however, that the low U.S. casualty figures—150 killed in action, about 450 wounded—"attest to the success of the operation's concept." In other words, the successful execution of the Hail Mary deception undeniably saved the lives of Coalition soldiers and pilots. And that seems to be a good reason to call the deception a success.

And so it has been with deception throughout history. Measuring success for an operation is not always an exact science. In some instances, like the deception hiding the evacuation of troops from Gallipoli, the evidence in the number of lives saved is clear. The success of Operation FORTITUDE, though clear, is not as easily measured.

But for such obviously successful deceptions, there are more deceptions that can be classified as *perhaps*. Perhaps the haversack ruse had an impact on the desert campaign. While Stonewall Jackson's maneuvers in the Shenandoah Valley didn't alter the outcome of the Civil War, perhaps they changed how the war was waged.

Finally, there is the tantalizing likelihood that historians know only a small part of what really happened with some of the deceptions in war. Surely there are deception operations that have yet to be made public. Some deception operations of World War II were classified for over fifty years because the U.S. didn't want to reveal its deception operations. After all, friends may become foes, and the U.S. might need to dust off those deceptions and use them again. And so the world of military deception remains shrouded in mystery and secrecy.

SOURCE NOTES

. . . .

Introduction: Deception Basics

pp. 1–2: "make false . . . military mission": Holt, pp. 53–54.

pp. 2–3: "planned measures . . . against an objective" and "planned measures . . . and act thereon": Daniel and Herbig, p. 53.

p. 3: "Cover conceals truth . . . induces action": Holt, p. 53.

p. 7: "un-American": Dewar, p. 190.

p. 7: "All warfare is based on deception": Sun Tzu.

Chapter 1: Early Deceptions

p. 16: "impetuous and bold": Alexander, p. 159.

p. 18: "clever stratagem . . . unlikely": Dewar, p. 27.

p. 18: "common tactic . . . in England": Dunnigan and Nofi, p. 73.

p. 19: "almost impregnable fortress": Alexander, p. 308.

p. 20: "most of the lower . . . be drawn out": Ibid.

p. 21: "band of eager volunteers": Ibid., p. 311.

p. 22: "It was a time . . . Wolfe wanted": Alan Salmon, "Two Great Soldiers," Combined Operations Command Memorial website, www .combinedops.com/Wolfe%27s%20Amphibious%20Assault%202.htm.

p. 22: "disintegrating . . . into the town": Alexander, p. 312.

pp. 22–23: "one of the most momentous battles in world history" and "produced the political . . . America emerged": Ibid., p. 306.

p. 23: "Always mystify, mislead, and surprise the enemy": Holt, p. 1.

p. 24: "watching Comanches . . . adjacent hills": Iain Standen, "Flags, Lanterns, Rockets and Wires: Signalling in the American Civil War," Signal Corps Association website, http://www.civilwarsignals.org/pages /signal/signalpages/standen.html.

pp. 28–29: "marched and countermarched . . . choreography" and "striking where least . . . had hit them": Holt, p. 1.

p. 30: "still somewhat apprehensive" and "You will give no . . . cover this city": "Hoodwinked During America's Civil War: Confederate Military

Deception," HistoryNet.com, http://www.historynet.com/hoodwinked
-during-americas-civl-war-confederate-military-deception.htm.

p. 30: "If I can deceive . . . the enemy": Alexander, p. 120.

p. 30: "see the westward . . . their destinations": Richard Baker, "The Lost
and Found Art of Deception," United States Army website, www.army
.mil/article/66819/the_lost_and_found_art_of_deception.

Chapter 2: Camouflage and Haversacks

p. 34: "working out the right . . . observation posts": Rankin, p. 113.

p. 35: "Secrecy in the affair . . . importance" and "the King . . .
Sandringham": Ibid., p. 118.

p. 35: "a structure . . . the enemy": "Observer's Post of Sheet Metal
Resembles Tree," *Popular Mechanics,* December 1917, www
.oldmagazinearticles.com/WW1_fake_Tree_Stump_Observation_Post.

pp. 35–36: "'lumps' on the outer . . . rough texture": "German
'Baumbeobachter' artillery observation post camouflaged as a tree,"
Australian War Memorial website, https://www.awm.gov.au/collection
/RELAWM04476/.

p. 42: "Everything that . . . to failure": Rankin, p. 104.

p. 43: more than 8.5 million killed . . . : "WWI Casualty and Death
Tables," *The Great War and the Shaping of the 20th Century,* PBS
website, http://www.pbs.org/greatwar/resources/casdeath_pop.html.

pp. 47–48: Casualties for both sides . . . : Edward Erickson, *Ordered to
Die: A History of the Ottoman Army in the First World War* (Westport, CT:
Greenwood, 2000), p. 137.

p. 48: "casualties of such . . . up to 50 percent": Michael Duffy, "Battles:
The Evacuation of Anzac Cove, Suvla Bay and Helles, 1915–16," First
World War.com, http://www.firstworldwar.com/battles/evacuation_dec15
.htm.

p. 49: "our chances of success . . . than useless": Dewar, p. 39.

p. 49: "bold plan . . . weaker force": Stanley, p. 176.

p. 49: "silent night withdrawal": Rankin, p. 39.

p. 51: "silent stunts": "The Evacuation of Anzac, December 1915,"
Australian Government, Department of Veterans' Affairs, Gallipoli and
the Anzacs website, www.gallipoli.gov.au/north-beach-and-the-sari-bair
-range/evacuation-of-anzac.php.

p. 50: "a live and let live policy was being adopted": "A Walk Around
14 Battlefield Sites: 14. Overlooking the North Beach at Walker's Ridge,"

Australian Government, Department of Veterans' Affairs, Gallipoli and the Anzacs website, www.gallipoli.gov.au/anzac-battlefield-sites-walk /site-14-walkers-ridge.php#!lightbox-uid-5.

p. 51: One group was ordered . . . A cricket match . . . : Ibid.

p. 51: Supplies and equipment were handled . . . : "The Evacuation of Anzac, December 1915," Australian Government, Department of Veterans' Affairs, Gallipoli and the Anzacs website, www.gallipoli.gov.au/north -beach-and-the-sari-bair-range/evacuation-of-anzac.php.

p. 51: "How silently . . . serpentine streak": Ibid.

p. 52: "drip rifle": "G01291," Australian War Memorial website, https:// www.awm.gov.au/collection/G01291/.

p. 53: "all the many . . . exaggerated": Stanley, p. 178.

p. 53: "successfully evacuated . . . from Helles," Rankin, p. 109.

p. 54: "echoed right through . . . lonely feeling": "The Evacuation of Anzac, December 1915," Australian Government, Department of Veterans' Affairs, Gallipoli and the Anzacs website, www.gallipoli.gov.au/north -beach-and-the-sari-bair-range/evacuation-of-anzac.php.

p. 56: "set off the charges . . . and shelling" and "more useful material . . . to Istanbul": Rankin, p. 109.

p. 56: "the successful end of a sad adventure": Ibid., p. 105.

p. 57: "heavily reliant upon . . . aircraft": Michael Duffy, "Battles: The Defence of the Suez Canal, 1915," First World War.com, http://www .firstworldwar.com/battles/suez.htm.

p. 57: "led to pressure . . . Palestine": "Palestine Campaign: Overview," New Zealand History website, http://www.nzhistory.net.nz/war/palestine -campaign/overview.

p. 58: "soldier of great vigour . . . his troops": David R. Woodward, "The Middle East During World War I," BBC website, http://www.bbc.co.uk /history/worldwars/wwone/middle_east_01.shtml.

p. 58: "(with both . . . 'The Bull'" and "close to desperation": Garfield, p. 16.

p. 58: "Jerusalem. By Christmas": Ibid., n252.

p. 61: "all sorts of nonsense . . . difficulties": Rankin, p. 165.

p. 61: "tidy sum . . . not intentional": Brown, p. 280.

p. 63: "218 guns . . . was imminent": Michael Duffy, "Battles: The Third Battle of Gaza, 1917," First World War.com, http://www.firstworldwar .com/battles/gaza3.htm.

p. 64: "muffle the thud . . . metal gear": Garfield, p. 22.

p. 64: "heroic magnitude": Ibid., p. 23.

p. 64: "a spectacular charge": Rankin, p. 166.

p. 65: "Christmas present for the British nation": "Palestine Campaign: Overview," New Zealand History website, http://www.nzhistory.net.nz/war/palestine-campaign/overview.

Chapter 3: Operation BERTRAM

p. 68: German tanks roared down . . . : Rankin, p. 459.

p. 70: allowing the British to take . . . : Brown, p. 50.

p. 70: "practice of deception . . . into an art": Dewar, p. 54.

p. 70: "deliberately vague . . . could stand for anything": Rankin, p. 462.

p. 71: "as quick as a ferret and about as likable": C. N. Trueman, "The Battle of El Alamein," History Learning website, http://www.historylearningsite.co.uk/world-war-two/war-in-north-africa/the-battle-of-el-alamein.htm.

pp. 72–73: "culled words . . . operational activities" and "fascinated with code . . . major operations": Gregory C. Sieminski, *Parameters,* Autumn 1995, 81–98, U.S. Army War College, Strategic Studies Institute website, http://strategicstudiesinstitute.army.mil/pubs/parameters/Articles/1995/sieminsk.htm.

p. 73–75: "personally approving . . . carried out," "well-sounding . . . operation," "her son was killed . . . 'Ballyhoo,'" and "inserted the words . . . about the invasion": Matthew Hickman, "How Military Operations Get Their Code Names," *Mental Floss,* September 8, 2011, http://mentalfloss.com/article/28711/how-military-operations-get-their-code-names.

p. 76: "fully automate . . . exercise terms" and "merely an automated . . . and storing": Gregory C. Sieminski, *Parameters,* Autumn 1995, 81–98, U.S. Army War College, Strategic Studies Institute website, http://strategicstudiesinstitute.army.mil/pubs/parameters/Articles/1995/sieminsk.htm.

p. 76: "actual code names . . . top secret": Art Pine, "Pentagon May Be Losing Operation Code Name Battle," *Los Angeles Times,* November 12, 1994, http://articles.latimes.com/print/1994-11-12/news/mn-61646_1_operation-torch.

pp. 78–79: "assess long-range prospects in the Northern front": Brown, p. 241.

p. 79: To help disseminate these lies . . . : Holt, p. 242.

p. 81: "concealed and revealed . . . master conjurer": Brown, p. 117.

p. 81: "Well, there it is. . . . got to!": Ibid., pp. 117–118.

p. 83: "A supply dump . . . apparent supply dump": Rankin, p. 522.

p. 84: "apparently camouflaged . . . to the south": Latimer, p. 83.

pp. 84–85: The engineers and soldiers working on it . . . : Brown, p. 120.

p. 87: Lieutenant Colonel Geoffrey Barkas . . . : Ibid., p. 118.

pp. 89–90: "rivers of blood" and "tank against tank": C. N. Trueman, "The Battle of El Alamein," History Learning website, http://www .historylearningsite.co.uk/world-war-two/war-in-north-africa battle-of-el -alamein.htm.

p. 90: thirty thousand Axis troops and about thirteen thousand Allied troops: Will Harney, "Battle of El Alamein," World War II Facts website, http://www.worldwar2facts.org/battle-of-el-alamein.html.

p. 90: "the Battle of Egypt . . . British victory": Rankin, p. 526.

p. 91: "the underbelly of the Axis": http://winstonchurchill.hillsdale.edu /soft-underbelly-fortress-europe/.

p. 91: "put the final seal of approval on deception": Holt, p. 244.

Chapter 4: Operation BODYGUARD

p. 93: "was claiming 10 million people a year": Macintyre, p. 1.

p. 93: "line of fortification . . . Great Wall of China": Brown, p. 3.

p. 95: "if the invaders . . . attack would fail": Macintyre, p. 1.

p. 97: "all the ideas . . . ideas and plans": Brown, p. 8.

p. 97: "intended to provide . . . sinister touches": Ibid., p. 5.

p. 97: "In war-time . . . bodyguard of lies": Howard, p. 105.

p. 98: "no avenue, however seemingly fantastic," "death ray," and "new and potent . . . nightfall": Budiansky, p. 77.

p. 100: "vaguely sinister term . . . operations in secrecy": Brown, p. 2.

p. 100: "probably his greatest . . . theory and practice": Ibid., p. 4.

p. 102: "an occasional act of thuggery": Brown, p. 5.

p. 102: "the ultimate secret . . . secret operations": Ibid., p. 8.

p. 103: "If [my enemy] . . . everywhere be weak": Sun Tzu.

Chapter 5: FORTITUDE NORTH

p. 109: "life-or-death implications": Holt, p. 556.

p. 110: the German military presence in Norway . . . : Brown, p. 462.

p. 111: "keep the native population in subjection" and "an insurance against invasion": Hesketh, p. 167.

p. 111: conqueror's mentality: Stephen E. Ambrose, "Eisenhower, the Intelligence Community, and the D-Day Invasion," *Wisconsin Magazine of History* 64, no. 4 (Summer 1981): 261–277, http://content .wisconsinhistory.org/cdm/ref/collection/wmh/id/35122.

p. 112: "no coincidence that . . . double agents": Crowdy, p. 9.

p. 112: "only several hundred . . . signals equipment": Ibid., p. 232.

p. 112: "volleys of Morse code . . . men": Macintyre, p. 224.

p. 112: "It's terrifically . . . a success": Breuer, *Hoodwinking Hitler*, p. 121.

p. 113: "main element in the plan . . . Fourth Army": Cruickshank, p. 10.

p. 118: "a gigantic volume of fictitious radio signaling": Ibid., p. 107.

p. 119: "April 12: Assault . . . amphibious exercise: Ibid., p. 106.

pp. 119–120: "0400 hours: Barrage . . . through Douglas": Ibid., pp. 107–108.

p. 121: "after all, a familiar British trick": Brown, p. 465.

p. 122: "an eclectic collection . . . to compromise": Dunnigan and Nofi, p. 236.

p. 122: "variously motivated . . . blackmail": Macintyre, p. 35.

p. 123: "by one means or another": Masterman, p. 2.

p. 123: "used defensively: . . . network in Britain": Macintyre, p. 4.

p. 123: "first attempt . . . supporting team" and "to plan their part . . . forces engaged": Hesketh, p. 71.

p. 124: "every single German . . . under his control": Macintyre, p. 4.

p. 124: "all the little lies . . . made up the big lie": Ibid., p. 5

p. 125: "safely be allowed to pass to the Germans": Masterman, p. 10.

p. 126: "A double agent cannot . . . often for years": Ibid., p. 9.

p. 126: "control and organize": Ibid., p. 15.

p. 128: "live the case . . . ears of his agent": Ibid., p. 22.

p. 130: "The great lie . . . hints, a mosaic": Macintyre, p. 231.

p. 130: "an imperative necessity" and "actually experience . . . to have done": Masterman, p. 19.

p. 131: "refused to continue to work" and "insufficient traffic": Ibid., appendix.

p. 131: "Brutus: October 1941 . . . May 1944": Hesketh, p. 65.

p. 133: "We owed our flying start . . . [double] agents": Ibid., p. 162.

p. 134: "hundreds, maybe thousands": Breuer, *Hoodwinking Hitler*, p. 124.

p. 135: "an enterprising capitalist . . . 'Fashion Avenue')" and "one way or another . . . these formations": Albert A. Nofi, "Deceit on D-Day: Outtakes from Victory and Deceit," Strategy Page, http://www.strategypage.com /articles/default.asp?target=ddaydeceit.htm&reader=long.

p. 135: "a shell on a dark background" and "completely unknown": Breuer, *Hoodwinking Hitler*, p. 125.

p. 136: "hundreds of twin-engine . . . Scottish airfields": Brown, p. 460.

p. 137: "may have contributed . . . the deception": Cruickshank, p. 104.

pp. 138–139: "always had good relations . . . do us harm," "must not continue . . . to prevent it," and "cost of maintaining . . . effort required": Hesketh, p. 166.

p. 139: "As time went on . . . in its reality": Macintyre, p. 225.

Chapter 6: FORTITUDE SOUTH

p. 141: "crown jewel of the Bodyguard deception": Donovan, p. 8.

p. 142: "largest, most elaborate . . . deception operations" and "years of experience . . . deceptive arts": Cruickshank, p. 170.

p. 145: "fake lighting schemes": Ibid.

p. 147: "media firestorm": Matt Soniak, FUSAG: The Ghost Army of World War II," *Mental Floss,* April 13, 2012, http://mentalfloss.com /article/30447/fusag-ghost-army-world-war-ii.

p. 147: "reprehensible" and "despicable": Brown, p. 473.

p. 148: "virtually the whole original FUSAG was fictitious": Cruickshank, p. 180.

p. 148: "elaborate masquerade on a colossal scale": Breuer, *Hoodwinking Hitler*, p. 113.

p. 150: "converted into an air defense training school" and "groups of rather odd, mainly middle-aged men": M. Smith, p. 1.

p. 150: "an overalertness . . . problems": Budiansky, p. 135.

p. 151: In 1941, the Government Codes and Cypher School advertised . . . than twelve minutes.: M. Smith, p. 81.

p. 152: "world's first semi-programmable electronic computer": "Strategic Ciphers," Bletchley Park website, http://www.bletchleypark.org.uk /content/hist/worldwartwo/stratciphers.rhtm.

p. 153: "My own conclusion . . . Mediterranean and Europe": Sir Harry Hinsley, "The Influence of ULTRA in the Second World War," CIX Online, Keith Lockstone home page, http://www.cix.co.uk/~klockstone /hinsley.htm.

p. 156: "business purposes . . . dangerously ill": Cruickshank, p. 173.

p. 156: "unprecedented step" and "distinctly un-British . . . Churchill included": Crowdy, p. 245.

pp. 156–157: "maximum concealment area," "would be hidden as far as was humanly possible," and "Tents must be . . . instead of white": Cruickshank, p. 176.

p. 157: "from the air . . . staging areas" and "blow-up tanks . . . quite real": Donovan, p. 10.

p. 158: "even sewage treatment farms": Brian John Murphy, "Patton's Ghost Army," *America in WWII,* December 2005, http://www .americainwwii.com/articles/pattons-ghost-army/.

p. 159: "blizzard of simulated radio traffic": Breuer, *Hoodwinking Hitler,* p. 116.

p. 160: "eight-inch-thick . . . transmissions": Brian John Murphy, "Patton's Ghost Army," *America in WWII,* December 2005, http://www .americainwwii.com/articles/pattons-ghost-army/.

p. 160: "mimic the traffic . . . wire recorders": Holt, p. 541.

p. 160: "13,358 phony messages . . . 230 a day": Ibid., p. 543.

pp. 160–161: "massive influx . . . citizenry" and "among young British women . . . Canadian troops": Breuer, *Hoodwinking Hitler,* p. 115.

p. 161: "Fakery had become . . . Fortitude and Quicksilver" and "an enormous film lot": Brown, p. 605.

p. 161: "conclusions about the direction . . . in the ports": Cruickshank, p. 177.

p. 162: "landing ships . . . oil drums": Brown, p. 603.

p. 162: "Galley fires were simulated . . . washing hung out": Cruickshank, p. 183.

p. 163: "an elaborate failure": Ibid., p. 182.

p. 163: "transparent fiction was kept up to the bitter end": Ibid., p. 183.

p. 164: "adjusted to focus attention on a false objective" and "drew attention . . . in that direction": Hesketh, p. 118.

p. 164: "twice as many visits . . . target area": Holt, p. 551.

pp. 164–165: "special work . . . extra tunneling" and "appropriate new wireless units will be opened up": Hesketh, p. 386.

p. 165: "workers on the ground . . . in a haze": Brian John Murphy, "Patton's Ghost Army," *America in WWII,* December 2005, http://www .americainwwii.com/articles/pattons-ghost-army/.

p. 165: "unconscionably slow": Holt, p. 551.

p. 166: "run up and down . . . taking off and landing" and "real looking planes . . . canvas and tubing": Donovan, p. 10.

p. 167: "butcher's bill would soar": Macintyre, p. 6.

p. 168: "All right . . . them have it!": Ibid., p. 316.

p. 169: "verbal flamethrower": Ibid., p. 322.

pp. 169–170: "After personal consultation . . . which is to say Berlin": Pujol and West, p. 200.

p. 170: "unless all the indications . . . will be fought": Levine, p. 199.

p. 170: "submit urgently . . . in these times": Pujol and West, p. 166.

p. 170: "hurtled up the chain of command": Macintyre, p. 325.

pp. 172–173: "combines the qualities . . . an extended period" and "no physical deception . . . dispensed with": Hesketh, p. 353.

Chapter 7: Deception After World War II

p. 177: "first military action of the Cold War": "Korean War," History.com, http://www.history.com/topics/korean-war.

p. 177: "utterly unprepared": "Korean War: Operation Chromite," HistoryNet.com, http://www.historynet.com/korean-war-operation -chromite.htm.

p. 180: "notoriously self-centered" and "rely upon strategic . . . odds against [him]": Ballard, p. 31.

pp. 180–181: "The very arguments . . . make such an attempt": Ballard, p. 33.

p. 182: "almost anticlimactic": "Korean War: Operation Chromite,"
HistoryNet.com, http://www.historynet.com/korean-war-operation
-chromite.htm.

p. 182: "believer in reconnaissance": Ballard, p. 32.

p. 182: "only lightly defended": "Korean War: Operation Chromite,"
HistoryNet.com, http://www.historynet.com/korean-war-operation
-chromite.htm.

p. 182: "We shall land at Inchon and I shall crush": Ballard, p. 34.

p. 184: "absolutely will not tolerate . . . invaded by imperialists,"
"sit back with folded . . . come to the border," and "a bald attempt to
blackmail the United Nations": Waters, p. 65.

p. 185: "nearly half a million . . . into North Korea": Dunnigan and Nofi,
p. 269.

p. 185: "every man, every gun . . . rested by day": Fehrenbach, p. 194.

p. 185: "was under orders to halt . . . engines went away" and "hundreds
of times . . . anything suspicious": Ibid., p. 195.

p. 186: "self-deception of the highest order": Dunnigan and Nofi, p. 270.

p. 186: "never be foolish . . . mechanized army": Ibid., p. 272.

p. 186: "prevailing color . . . brown villages": Manchester, p. 545.

p. 187: "well aware of the capabilities . . . intelligence": Waters, p. 69.

p. 187: "even marched during daytime . . . tell the difference": Lee,
p. 160.

p. 187: "conventional means . . . supply dumps": Hastings, p. 137.

p. 187: "wrecked several South Korean . . . regiment as well": Dunnigan
and Nofi, p. 271.

p. 188: "This was good advice . . . wasn't enough" and "popping out of
the hills": Ibid., p. 271.

p. 191: "tired of coups": "The Vietnam War: America Commits,
1961–1964," The History Place website, http://www.historyplace.com
/unitedstates/vietnam/index-1961.html.

pp. 191–192: the 4.2 million tons of bombs dropped . . . in World War II:
Dunnigan and Nofi, p. 273.

pp. 192–194: "from which a great weight . . . area of operations," "used
deception to such good effect," "an enemy tactic . . . un-American," and
"masters of subterfuge": Dewar, p. 190.

p. 195: "thousands of South Vietnamese . . . headquarters" and "turned
out to be . . . sympathizers": Dunnigan and Nofi, p. 278.

p. 196: "let go with some firepower": Ibid., p. 281.

p. 196: "increase the insecurity . . . South Vietnam" and "establish a base . . . operations": Shultz, p. 28.

p. 196: "were either captured . . . after they got there": Ibid., p. 90.

p. 197: "total of 72 . . . separate operations" and "major escalation of America's secret war": Ibid., p. xiii.

p. 197: "complex deception program . . . support for the VC": Monroe, p. 124.

p. 197: "highly secret new . . . these operations": Shultz, p. 40.

p. 198: "All the teams that OP 34 . . . Ministry of the Interior": Ibid., p. 91.

p. 198: "run back against . . . the SOG": Ibid., p. 92.

p. 198: "a fixation on subversion . . . take its toll," "cranked up . . . different purpose," and "to play hardball": Ibid., p. 112.

p. 199: "create the impression . . . in North Vietnam": Monroe, p. 124.

p. 200: "most zealous Communists": Gillespie, p. 140.

p. 201: "it was highly likely . . . that we planted": Shultz, p. 118.

p. 201: "a completely scripted . . . affair" and "special ceremony . . . secret brotherhood": Ibid., p. 115.

p. 202: "clearly was having the intended effect" and "feeling the heat . . . threat of subversion": Ibid., p. 124.

p. 202: "revealed an increasing . . . spies, and espionage": Ibid., p. 330.

p. 205: "The whole notion is to bypass . . . and to them": Dempsey, p. 15.

p. 206: "backbone for its battlefield communications system": Boyle.

p. 206: "maximum of one receiver . . . 180 men" and "more than 100,000 . . . nine-man squad": Cordesman, p. 200.

p. 207: "godsend for ground troops . . . by the system" and "find and feed soldiers . . . among the dunes": Colleen A. Nash, "Chart Page: GPS Success in Desert Storm," *Air Force Magazine* 74, no. 8 (August 1991): 35.

p. 208 : Rumaila, the largest oil field in Iraq . . . barrels of oil: Christopher Helman, "The World's Biggest Oil Reserves," *Forbes,* January 21, 2010, http://www.forbes.com/2010/01/21/biggest-oil-fields-business-energy-oil -fields.html.

p. 208: five thousand tanks and seven thousand military aircraft and helicopters: Rebecca Grant, "Desert Storm," *Air Force Magazine* 94, no. 1 (January 2011).

p. 210: more than $53 billion: Richard W. Murphy, "Persian Gulf War," *Grolier Multimedia Encyclopedia,* http://teacher.scholastic.com /scholasticnews/indepth/upfront/grolier/Persian_Gulf_War.htm.

p. 210: About 70 percent of the nearly one million troops . . . from the U.S.: "Gulf War Coalition Forces: Countries Compared," NationMaster .com, http://www.nationmaster.com/country-info/stats/Military/Gulf -War-Coalition-Forces.

p. 213: "an amphibious feint . . . reinforce the threat": Breitenbach, p. 7.

p. 213: "precisely reinforced the deceptive scheme": Ibid., p. 17.

pp. 213–214: "faced units at only 50 to 70 percent of their original strength": "Schwarzkopf's Strategy," *Los Angeles Times,* February 28, 1991, http://articles.latimes.com/print/1991-02-28/news/ mn-2880_1_iraqi-forces.

p. 214: "dug-in Iraqis . . . Kuwaiti border": Ibid.

p. 214: "huge mass of 20,000 . . . nearly a week": Dunnigan and Nofi, p. 320.

p. 214: "western wastelands": Ibid., p. 319.

p. 215: "were not used to operating in the desert," "had regarded it as such for thousands of years," and "would revolutionize desert navigation": Ibid., p. 320.

p. 215: "considered armor movement . . . navigational problems": D. Smith, p. 17.

p. 216: "incapable of massing . . . without features": Breitenbach, p. 11.

p. 216: "within limits, the greater . . . being believed": Ibid., p. 16.

p. 217: "little resistance": "Schwarzkopf's Strategy," *Los Angeles Times,* February 28, 1991, http://articles.latimes.com/1991-02-28/news/mn -2880_1_iraqi-forces.

p. 217: "each commander . . . be overlooked": Breitenbach, p. 9.

p. 218: "an impressive-looking . . . border": Dunnigan and Nofi, p. 318.

p. 218: "attack into the teeth of the defense" and "gave them what they wanted": Breitenbach, p. 10.

p. 219: "a solid wall across the north" and "The gates are closed": "Schwarzkopf's Strategy," *Los Angeles Times,* February 28, 1991, http:// articles.latimes.com/1991-02-28/news/mn-2880_1_iraqi-forces.

p. 220: "attest to the success of the operation's concept": D. Smith, p. 19.

BIBLIOGRAPHY

Alexander, Bevin. *How Wars Are Won: The 13 Rules of War from Ancient Greece to the War on Terror.* New York: Crown, 2002.

Ambrose, Stephen E. *D-Day, June 6, 1944: The Climactic Battle of World War II.* New York: Simon & Schuster, 1994.

Anderson, David L. *The Columbia Guide to the Vietnam War.* New York: Columbia University Press, 2002.

Andrew, Christopher. *Defend the Realm: The Authorized History of MI5.* New York: Knopf, 2009.

Ballard, John R. "Operation Chromite: Counterattack Inchon." *Joint Force Quarterly,* Spring/Summer 2001, 31–36. http://www.dtic.mil/cgi -bin/GetTRDoc?AD=ADA527749.

Betts, Richard K. *Surprise Attack: Lessons for Defense Planning.* Washington, DC: Brookings Institution, 1982.

Boyle, Alan. "GPS Satellite Network Goes to War." NBC News.com, March 19, 2003. http://www.nbcnews.com//id/3078694/# .U2eq9MfR3cl.

Breitenbach, Daniel L. "Operation Desert Deception: Operation Deception in the Ground Campaign." Newport, RI: U.S. Naval War College, 1991.

Breuer, William B. *Hoodwinking Hitler: The Normandy Deception.* Westport, CT: Praeger, 1993.

———. *Shadow Warriors: The Covert War in Korea.* New York: Wiley, 1996.

Brown, Anthony Cave. *Bodyguard of Lies.* New York: Harper & Row, 1975.

Budiansky, Stephen. *Blackett's War.* New York, Knopf, 2013.

Clodfelter, Michael. *Vietnam in Military Statistics: A History of the Indochina Wars, 1772–1991.* Jefferson, NC: McFarland, 1995.

Cordesman, Anthony H. *The Iraq War: Strategy, Tactics, and Military Lessons.* Westport, CT: Praeger, 2003.

Crowdy, Terry. *Deceiving Hitler: Double Cross and Deception in World War II.* New York: Osprey, 2008.

Cruickshank, Charles. *Deception in World War II.* New York: Oxford University Press, 1979.

Daniel, Donald C., and Katherine L. Herbig, eds. *Strategic Military Deception.* New York: Pergamon, 1982.

Dempsey, Dale. "Ground War, Daring Attack Shatters Iraq's Battered Defense." *Dayton Daily News,* March 14, 1991, p. 15.

Dewar, Michael. *The Art of Deception in Warfare.* Devon, England: David & Charles, 1989.

Donovan, Michael J. "Strategic Deception: Operation Fortitude." Carlisle Barracks, PA: U.S. Army War College, 2002.

Dunnigan, James F., and Albert A. Nofi. *Victory and Deceit: Dirty Tricks at War.* New York: Morrow, 1995.

Fehrenbach, T. R. *This Kind of War: A Study in Unpreparedness.* New York: Macmillan, 1963.

Fishel, Edwin C. *The Secret War for the Union: The Untold Story of Military Intelligence in the Civil War.* Boston: Houghton Mifflin, 1996.

Garfield, Brian. *The Meinertzhagen Mystery: The Life and Legend of a Colossal Fraud.* Washington, DC: Potomac, 2007.

Gillespie, Robert M. *Black Ops, Vietnam: The Operational History of MACVSOG.* Annapolis, MD: Naval Institute Press, 2011.

Hastings, Max. *The Korean War.* New York: Simon & Schuster, 1987.

Hesketh, Roger. *Fortitude: The D-Day Deception Campaign.* Woodstock, NY: Overlook, 2000.

Holt, Thaddeus. *The Deceivers: Allied Military Deception in the Second World War.* New York: Scribner, 2004.

Howard, Michael. *British Intelligence in the Second World War.* London: HMSO, 1990.

Latimer, Jon. *Deception in War.* Woodstock, NY: Overlook, 2001.

Lee, Bong. *The Unfinished War: Korea.* New York: Algora, 2003.

Levine, Joshua. *Operation Fortitude.* London: Collins, 2011.

Lewin, Ronald. *Ultra Goes to War: The First Account of World War II's Greatest Secret Based on Official Documents.* New York: McGraw-Hill, 1978.

Macintyre, Ben. *Double Cross: The True Story of the D-day Spies.* New York: Crown, 2012.

Manchester, William. *American Caesar: Douglas MacArthur, 1880–1964.* Boston: Little, Brown, 1978.

Masterman, J. C. *The Double-Cross System: The Incredible True Story of How Nazi Spies Were Turned into Double Agents.* New York: Lyons, 2000.

Monroe, James D. "Deception: Theory and Practice." Monterey, CA: Naval Postgraduate School, 2012.

Montagu, Ewen. *The Man Who Never Was.* Philadelphia: Lippincott, 1954.

Pujol, Juan, with Nigel West. *Garbo.* London: Weidenfeld and Nicolson, 1985.

Rankin, Nicholas. *Churchill's Wizards: The British Genius for Deception, 1914–1945.* London: Faber and Faber, 2008.

Shultz, Richard H. Jr. *The Secret War Against Hanoi: Kennedy's and Johnson's Use of Spies, Saboteurs, and Covert Warriors in North Vietnam.* New York: HarperCollins, 1999.

Smith, Douglas V. "Military Deception and Operational Art." Newport, RI: U.S. Naval War College, 1993.

Smith, Michael. *Station X: The Codebreakers of Bletchley Park.* London: Channel 4 Books, 1998.

Stanley, Peter. *Quinn's Post: Anzac, Gallipoli.* Sydney: Allen & Unwin, 2005.

Sun Tzu. *The Art of War.* Translated by Lionel Giles. http://classics.mit.edu/Tzu/artwar.html.

Waters, Lonn Augustine. "Secrecy, Deception and Intelligence Failure: Explaining Operational Surprise in War." Master's thesis, MIT, 2005. http://hdl.handle.net/1721.1/33710.

IMAGE CREDITS

. . . .

p. 66	M40 single-decal army helmet with three-color spray camouflage courtesy of Ken Niewiarowicz
p. 74	*Operation Jericho* by Phillip E. West. Reprinted by permission of SWA Fine Arts.
p. 85	(top) Photo provided by the Imperial War Museum. Reprinted with permission.
	(bottom) Image courtesy of Richard Stokes, from his website Jasper Maskelyne, maskelynemagic.com
p. 89	Photo provided by the Imperial War Museum. Reprinted with permission.
p. 92	British World War II M1942 Windproof brushstroke camouflage pattern courtesy of Eric. H. Larson
p. 96	"Conference of the Big Three at Yalta makes final plans for the defeat of Germany. Prime Minister Winston S. Churchill, President Franklin D. Roosevelt, and Premier Josef Stalin." February 1945. 111-SC-260486. National Archives Identifier: 531340.
p. 99	"Three soldiers of the United States Army sit in place at a radar used by the 90th Coast Artillery in Casablanca, French Morocco." June 19, 1943. 111-SC-223413. National Archives Identifier: 531325.
p. 104	"Down the ramp of a Coast Guard landing barge." June 6, 1944. 111-SC-223413. National Archives Identifier: 531325.
p. 108	German World War II Wehrmacht Splittermuster camouflage pattern courtesy of Eric H. Larson
p. 114	Courtesy of the www.w1tp.com Telegraph Museum
p. 116	Library of Congress item no. 2006691784
p. 136	National Archives, U.K., AIR 20/4349. Reprinted with permission.
p. 140	U.S. World War II M1942 green poncho spot camouflage pattern courtesy of Eric H. Larson
p. 146	Library of Congress item no. 2005688170
p. 151	© Bletchley Park Trust
p. 158	© Imperial War Museum (H 42531)
p. 162	Photo provided by the Imperial War Museum. Reprinted with permission.

p. 174   U.S. six-color "day desert" camouflage pattern courtesy of Eric H. Larson

p. 181   Library of Congress item no. 2004679777

p. 183   U.S. Department of the Army

pp. 192–193   Associated Press

p. 211   *General Norman Schwarzkopf.* November 9, 1998. 330-CFD-DA-SC-92-06419. National Archives Identifier 647068.

INDEX

· · · · · · ·